UK Quilters United
by a second thread

The quilt which started UK Quilters United, made by Nina

Cover image: Rainbow Bargello by Juliet Nice

UK Quilters United
by a second thread

Inspirational stories written by
members of the Facebook group
UK Quilters United

Nina Danielsson

UK Quilters United
by a second thread

First edition, 2019
Collated, edited and published
by Nina Danielsson
www.bossyoz.com
ISBN 978-1-07-207159-4

To Mamma
who introduced me to sewing

Table of contents

Foreword

Our second book!

So much has happened since Julie Passey collected stories from the members of UK Quilters United back around our first birthday in 2015 and turned them into a book, UK Quilters United by a common thread. Since then, we have welcomed many thousands of new members. We have created almost a dozen Facebook sub-groups covering all aspects of quilting, as well as social groups, and we even have a professionally managed website. We unleashed a monster and it's taking over the United Kingdom and reaching its tentacles into the rest of the world as well.

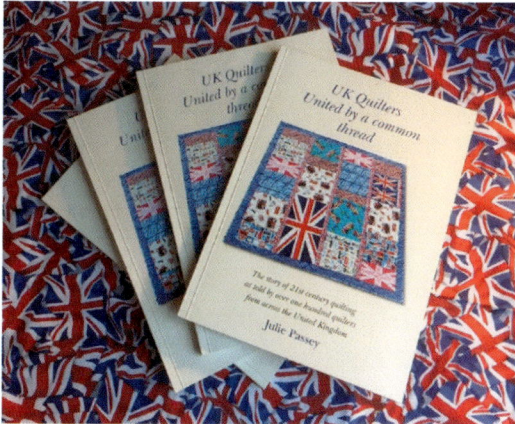

The first edition of our first book, by and about UK Quilters United

As quilters and anyone coming into contact with quilters already know, quilts are a joy, a hug and love in fabric form. We quilt not just for ourselves, but to share that love and joy with others. The stories in this book are an extension to this.

To create some structure, the stories have been grouped into four sections. The first section is about the UK Quilters United Facebook group and our website. In the second section our members share their quilting journeys and in the third section, we find out how quilting has been a great support through sometimes rather challenging times. The fourth section includes stories on how quilting has provided a way to change people's lives; be it starting a business, changing lifestyle or travelling the world.

Huge thank you to all our amazing writers and a special mention to Jeanne Carlin, Ruth Burns Warrens, Margaret Attfield and Linda Lane Thornton for their expert knowledge of the English language and eminent proof-reading skills.

Please enjoy these stories and the beautiful work of our members.

Juliet Nice and Nina Danielsson
Founders of UK Quilters United
June 2019

Facebook: www.facebook.com/groups/ukquiltersunited
Website: ukqu.co.uk

Rainbow Bargello, by Juliet

Cornish wonky crosses, by Nina

UK Quilters United

There was a young lady called Juliet
Who once had a dream...oh! you bet!
Not about Romeo
But 'cos she loved to sew
Founded UKQU on the net

Being an Admin

By Mo Jones

After 'meeting' for the first time in a global quilt group, Juliet Nice and Nina Danielsson agreed that a Facebook group for quilters living in the United Kingdom was needed. That very afternoon, the Facebook group UK Quilters United was set up by the two of them.

I was the first admin who came on board from the UK members who had joined the group. Juliet and Nina needed someone to take over the Members' Locations list, to help other members finding quilters in their local area. As Juliet admitted, she is hopeless at geography.

Six admins looking after 16,000 members

Later on, Maggie Howell come on board and she took over the Members' Locations list, while I started looking after getting prizes for our competitions. We tend to hold these when we reach milestones such as big round numbers of members joining our great group and for every birthday at the end of January. It is amazing that in 2019 we celebrated five years and reaching nearly 16,000 members. What an achievement!

We now have six admins; after Maggie, Diana Hibble stepped up, shortly followed by Carol Munro. We do our best to keep our members happy in the group by providing comments on posts, as well as deleting non-quilting related pictures and chats.

Following votes by our members, we have a strict 'no advertising and no self-promotion' rule in the group, but we do get some funny members who like to advertise sunglasses, etc.

The only time we allow advertising is when we have competitions. I then post the prizes offered by our members, naming the shops who donated the prize. This is usually done as a teaser post with a photo showing what could be won when entering the competition.

We now have lots of different sub-groups for our members to join, providing places for social chat, facilitating swaps, continuing development and much more, and at least one main group admin is also an admin in each sub-group.

Spreading the word whilst supporting charity

Living in Cornwall, I set up a separate Facebook group for anyone living locally. During 2018, I asked our Cornwall members if they would like to make a quilt to raffle for the Cornwall Air Ambulance. I had a fantastic response and we set to making the quilt as well as trying to find ways to sell raffle tickets.

I contacted the organisers for both the Craft4Crafters Show and The West Country Quilt & Textile Show (WCQ&TS) asking if we could have spaces at their shows. So far, we have had galleries or stands at shows in Bristol, Exeter and Shepton Mallett. So popular were our displays, that WCQ&TS Bristol and Craft4Crafters have given us bigger galleries at their shows this year. As an added bonus, we have also been able to sell our UK Quilters United merchandise at the shows.

Having successfully sold raffle tickets throughout the year, at the beginning of March 2019, some of the Cornwall group went to the Cornwall Air Ambulance Headquarters where the crew on shift pulled the winning tickets and the raffle quilt made an amazing £3,065.50. It was a great day!

Continuing the promotion of our groups

Looking ahead and trying to find a new way to interact with and engage visitors coming to our exhibition stands, I asked the UKQU Postcard Swap Facebook group to help me get more interest in our galleries by making fabric postcards for us to display. The response was tremendous and I am pleased to say that the postcards continue to bring lots more people to our galleries at the various shows and we are continuously receiving lots of lovely comments. We are making postcards on different themes for the various shows.

As well as helping running our main UK Quilters United Facebook group and the Cornwall group, I have opened a sub-group for members who are interested in having their work on display in our exhibition galleries. This year we will exhibit A4-sized quilts as well as postcards. If you like to join in, just search for **UKQU** Show Galleries on Facebook and you can join us.

Volunteering to be an admin of UK Quilters United has helped me meet lots of new people. As well as looking after a few different UKQU Facebook sub-groups, I look after the competitions and promote our great group at shows in the south west of England.

Seeing the success and how much fun we're having in the south west, I would highly recommend other members located around the country to get spaces at shows to help promote UK Quilters United elsewhere.

The raffle quilt supporting the Cornwall Air Ambulance

PS. If you would like to read my story in our first book, UK Quilters, United by a common thread, you'll find it in the Devon section, although I live in Cornwall.

Find me online at ukqu.co.uk/members/mojo/blog

My quilting journey with UKQU

By Jacquie Lawrence

My journey with UKQU started quite soon after the Facebook group was launched. Oh my, what a long way I've come! Don't get me wrong, I still cut strips of fabric at the wrong length, forget to reverse appliqué designs ready for bonding and don't get me started with Foundation Paper Piecing (FPP).

The many Facebook groups provide a variety of challenges

A a member of the many Facebook groups I've made seaside blocks, triangles, circles and houses (with FPP) in the Block Swap group, some beautiful postcards in the Postcard group and stunning mini quilts in the Mini Swap group. Each time I've taken part I've learnt something new or passed on a bit of knowledge to someone else. But, most importantly, I have had fun along the way. The Continuing Development group has had a diverse range of topics and techniques discussed and new knowledge passed on. We even have a 'virtual' choir in the Block Swap group. It's a good job we take part remotely though, as I gather we would sound more like cats on hot tin roofs.

Lone stitcher with supportive online friends

My quilting and sewing have helped me get through some difficult times, just like many others in the various groups. I am a lone stitcher for many reasons, but having so many people who I consider to be friends there for me on Facebook, is nothing short of a miracle.

We encourage each other and we are always on hand with tips and hints. If you want to chat about life in general there is the Social group too

I never knew when I joined UKQU that I would be able to create quilts and sew amazing gifts to the standard that I do. I have even had enough courage to send a quilt off to an exhibition last year. The judges' comments blew me away. The judges commented that my work showed stunningly detailed quilting and good choice of colours. The sub categories were scored good and very good as well as each judge awarded one excellent, for "execution of quality". I have to thank the members of the group for their expert advice which they have given me so willingly.

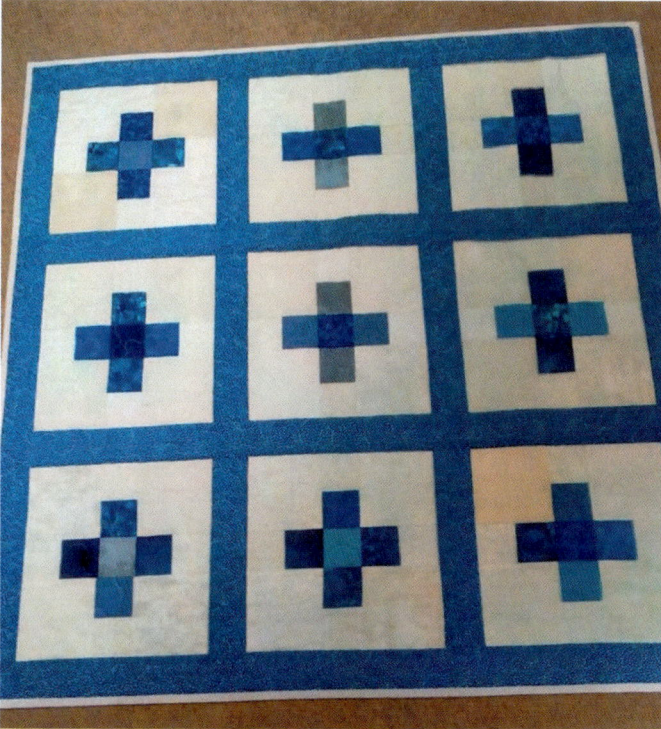

Quilt made with blocks from the Block Swap group

Leaving my rock for an adventure at Festival of Quilts

The most amazing part of my quilting journey with UKQU was joining in the fun at the Festival of Quilts last year. I had a significant birthday and set myself a few challenges to do before the big day arrived. Now, I mentioned earlier that I am a lone stitcher; well, that's because I can't cope with lots of company and I get exhausted easily. I also DON'T do travelling. Living on a rock in the Bay of St Malo, in other words the Channel Islands, I have to get on a plane or a boat. This creates panic for me and I think, "Oh, why am I doing this!?"

I arrived at Birmingham airport, was picked up by Juliet, the original founder of the Facebook group. We checked in, left our luggage and made our way to the NEC. The thought that immediately came to mind was, "OMG! What was all the worry about?"

The festival was amazing and my UKQU Facebook buddies accepted me and we had so much fun together. It was like we'd known each other, in person, for years. We also met up with other members of the group, each day, and it was magic. Each and everyone are now life-long friends.

Making life-long friends

Will we ever meet, in person, again? I don't know and to be honest I don't mind. We are all travelling the same road. Sewing and creating while being amongst friends. We are passing on our makes to friends, family and charitable causes.

Quilting eases the mind, definitely not the pocket (just in case anyone is under any illusions) but is well worth it.

The quilt I made for my partner in the 2018 mini quilt swap

The UKQU website

By Sylvia Priest

June 2014 is the date I first joined UK Quilters United on Facebook. Back then there were less members; mostly we shared the quilts we put together and almost everyone knew everyone else. That friendly little group grew steadily to where it is today. To me it's still the best social group on Facebook and one of the friendliest and happiest quilting groups I have had the pleasure to be part of.

Spotting an opportunity

In the Facebook group, as well as sharing the quilts we made, we shared ideas, information, knowledge, hints and tips. One evening in 2017 Juliet (the originator of the Facebook group) and I put our heads together to work out how it all might be collated in a way that would make it simple and easy for everyone to find what they were looking for. But more than that, in a way which would help and support the retail quilt market out there - our UK bricks and mortar local quilt shops as well as the UK based online retailers. A keen part of the website has always been to support the sector at all levels. So, the result of that chat now manifests itself in the website, ukqu.co.uk.

Taking the plunge

Resolution, my own company, is made up of professional video producers and website developers and it was decided to create the website everyone knows today. Resolution is a brand specialist too and the UKQU branding was developed first. The making of any website does not happen overnight, and we were doing this work around our regular day job, with lots of sleepless nights whilst bugs were ironed out, layouts agreed, beta testing the new pages and the programming is an art in itself. I am proud of my staff and without their efforts it could not have been done.

Six months later we launched the new website to a waiting audience and held our breath. The website is constantly evolving, with content increasing daily thanks to the amazing contributions from voluntary bloggers, fondly known as the Bloggerati.

Little did Juliet and Nina know when they started the Facebook group back in 2014 that there would be such a dynamic website which is rapidly becoming the reference point for patterns, advice, block libraries, mystery quilts, quilt news, product reviews, viewpoints, an extensive directory and a small, but growing online retail section.

One year on, busier than ever

January 2019 saw the first anniversary of the website, alongside the fifth anniversary of the Facebook group, with the website membership and visitor numbers growing daily. There are new avenues still to be explored and developed, and we hope the Facebook group members will continue to visit and appreciate the content on the website. The exciting part is the number of new people who visit and go on to join the diverse group of members in the social group too.

A main feature of the website has been the regular quilt competitions. These were only possible with the support of Grosvenor Shows and the prizes donated by all the sponsors. Throughout the Autumn of 2019 the winners are on display in the first, of what is hoped will be a continuing relationship with these major Quilt Show events. For the first time the 20 winning quilts, as well as our Sew a Row, Fire and Ice quilts (which were designed exclusively by the Bloggerati) and the Gulliver series will tour the UK for everyone to see for themselves - so not just as pictures online! Who could have imagined even a year ago that there would be a significant exhibition of member's quilts at the Great Northern Quilt Show? There are also six events, ending with the Springfield Christmas Show in Spalding, and many of the stallholders at these events are often featured within the website.

UKQU.co.uk and our supporters

The support from the UK quilting marketplace has been marvellous, and we are supported by our regular sponsors, including Janome, Barnyarns, Makower UK, Lewis and Irene, The Cotton Craft Co., EQS, Groves, Gutermann, Vliseline, and the British Patchwork and Quilting Magazine who we are sure you will agree are well known brands in the quilting and patchwork sector.

During our first year, 2018, we gave away over £1000 worth of prizes plus two Janome high-end sewing machines. In 2019, the donated prizes are growing and we are giving away four more Janome machines and already the prizes are surpassing those of our first year. We are also working with independent designers and pattern makers to offer exclusive quilt ideas to our members.

Influencing the UK quilting sector

The website, ukqu.co.uk is starting to influence the quilting sector in ways we could not have imagined. It's hard work, without a doubt, but one thing I do know, I am proud to be able to say I am part of it all. Would I do it again? In a heartbeat!

Find me online at ukqu.co.uk/members/sylviapriest/blog

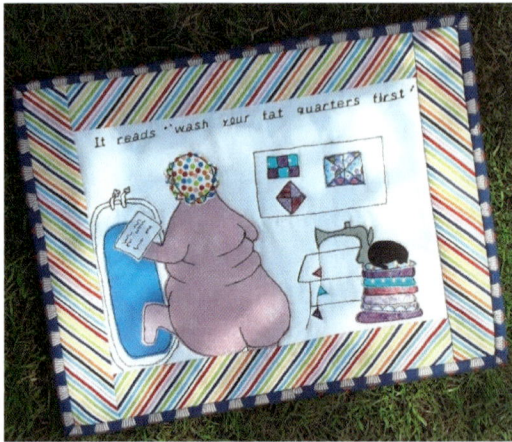

Postcard made by Lyn Butler, one of the Bloggerati

Finding quilty friends

By Sally Dodsworth

Although I love sitting at my machine and find the whole quilting process very relaxing, it can sometimes be a rather lonely experience. However, to my great delight I have found out it doesn't have to be so; let me explain…

Coming to live in Cornwall ten years ago meant I had to start again finding friends to craft with. A couple of colleagues at work had crafty interests and they would occasionally come over and join me for the afternoon, but somehow it felt like something was still missing and things never really took off.

Crafting with company

Then, one day, three or four years ago, I decided I wanted to learn how to sew a dress, to try something new. I invited a dressmaking friend to assist and she patiently… very patiently helped me make it. The finished result was a disaster (my doing, not hers!). But it started a monthly crafty afternoon where the two of us would sit and sew or quilt or crochet or knit or whatever took our fancy. If the weather was nice, we would sit outside and at the end of every session we always finished by arranging our next meeting. Throughout the months, we tried to get others to join us and occasionally someone would come, but our group still remained just the two of us.

Finding UK Quilters United

Meanwhile I had joined UK Quilters United on Facebook and I was thoroughly enjoying the online company and support. At one point I saw a call for quilters in Cornwall to meet up. My friend and I jumped at the opportunity and went to a first meeting, where we found to our great delight that the instigator of this group was our neighbour, living within a five minute drive of both of us.

The Cornwall group for UK Quilters United has monthly meetings, alternating between two fabric shops (Sew and Fabric in St Austell and Painters in Liskeard). It is a great time for like-minded people to get together, share ideas, show their work and just have a good old chin wag. The group celebrated its first birthday earlier in 2019 and has just finished a charity quilt raising money for the air ambulance (please see Mo Jones' story)…a massive achievement and we have also had a couple of days dedicated to making Linus quilts.

Quilty friends online and in real life

In addition to our regular monthly meetings, a group of seven of us have met up on a few different occasions to have a couple of sewing days – one of which involved a Christmas lunch and a secret Santa, and the other a day spent learning the technique of rust dying.

As an added bonus, our little monthly crafty afternoon now has three regular members, all of us living very close to each other.

I love the time spent with my new quilty friends and the online chats and banter make up for when we can't get to meet in person…long may it last!

My Raggedy Ruff BOM.
I took some finished blocks to share during the first meeting of the Cornwall UKQU group. A year later I was able to take in the finished quilt for the show and tell.

Spreading the nerd

By Carolyn Gibbs

I had become interested in patchwork and quilting when my children were small, and went on to teach it at Sheffield College, local shops and to various groups around the country, developing my own style, techniques and range of traditional style patterns. However, most of this activity got put on the back burner when I went back to what my husband called a "real job" teaching chemistry to international students. Better paid employment did provide the income to start an antique quilt collection though.

When I finally dropped down to part-time at work, I was able to get back to doing what I loved, and (with the help of my wonderfully techie daughter, Rachel), started a Facebook Page, and a website (link at end), but not many people found it......

Swirling stripes mug rug

The black hole that is the UKQU Facebook group

I can't remember how I found the UKQU Facebook group, but I was soon ~~wasting~~ spending hours looking at lovely quilts, and writing what I hoped were helpful comments, when people were asking for help and advice. Once a teacher, always a teacher….. Then in September 2017, a few months after I had joined, I read a post by Juliet Nice:

> "Have you ever considered sharing your quilting experience on a bigger scale? I am looking for members with experience of designing and writing patterns, writing blogs, making video tutorials and lots, lots more for our new UKQU website. Give Sylvia Priest a PM with your experience/qualifications/links to previous work. We're looking for everyone that can contribute, whether you want to write patterns or be a video star!"

Well, that sounded fun! And it would be a great chance to reach a wider range of quilters.

So, I became one of the original band of bloggers on the website, ukqu.co.uk, when it started in January 2018.

Silent star quilt block

My blogs on ukqu.co.uk

I have written about antique quilts a couple of times, but most of my posts seem to end up in the Hints & Tips section, as I enjoy writing about techniques and explaining how to avoid problems. My approach could definitely be described as "nerdy" which I suppose reflects my scientific background and liking for order and pattern; Pressing for Perfect Points, Success with Stripes, Colour and Contrast – I seem to like alliteration as well.

I know that accuracy, planning and fiddling with things until they are 'right' is not the way everyone likes (or needs) to do their patchwork and quilting. But there do seem to be plenty of quilters who leave comments saying how helpful they find my posts – so I shall go on "spreading the nerd" to support them in their pursuit of precise patchwork and quality quilting.

Find me online at www.carolyngibbsquilts.co.uk

Always aim for the perfect point

Quilting journeys

Memories, hopes and happiness

By Margaret Attfield

Looking back, I was probably a blinking nuisance as a child. Endlessly enthusiastic, always keen to learn, continually ready to ask questions, I soaked up knowledge like a sponge, and then demanded more. I realise this, because my English teacher once handed me a thick hardback book with no illustrations, small print and said:

"There. Read that. That should keep you quiet for a bit".

It was the first book of Tolkien's Lord of the Rings. I was eleven years old. It was in 1962.

I am bored...

So, it was not surprising that, when it was too wet to play outside, and I had read all my library books, and painted enough to decorate the National Gallery, I would be at a loss. My mother's usual remedy for boredom was effective - housework. If you got into a squabble with siblings, you got jobs to do in the house - separately. Floor polishing, furniture polishing, bed making, fetching carrots and onions from the shop, bringing in a bucket of coal... If you were bored, you got a job to do. Unsurprisingly, we were rarely bored. We didn't fight a lot, either, now that I think of it....

But on one occasion I must have been a particular nuisance, because she gave me a needle, pink and green Anchor embroidery thread, and a printed linen sampler a few inches square, and showed me how to do cross stitch. Then, row completed, she showed me how to feather stitch. And so on. That was my first effort at sewing. I think I was six. Before long, I was no longer hanging at her elbow threading her needles and watching her sew on the treadle Jones that made all our clothes. I was taking my first steps at sewing.

The sewing machine had been a thank you gift when my parents first settled in our home town, from the old man across the road for her time looking after his shop when he needed to make a delivery. And on it, she dressed my brothers and me.

Learning from mum, creating my own outfits

I always had up to date dresses. My mum had spent the war in London, and hats she made dressed every woman at her wartime wedding. Looking back at the photos, I see myself in a satin dress which I remember was pink (I was three or four), and a Christmas dress of black, brown and yellow Viyella tartan with a white collar; certainly the first "American style" to be seen in our neighbourhood.

By the time I was ten, I had completed two 2-piece outfits with box pleated skirts, neck facings, waistbands and darts good enough to wear to church. One was turquoise silk (rayon) brocade or damask, and the other was a bright red, blue and yellow border print in glazed cotton. They may not have been expertly made, but I was proud of them. How much my mum finished for me without my knowledge I can't say, but, knowing that in her nineties she would undo and restitch the fumbling attempts of her hapless friend in her little group of quilters, I suspect it was more than I knew. But I never felt I was a failure even though her mantra was "Slapdash. A thing worth doing is worth doing well".

Dark Viyella dresses with white collars and black tights were very new when I was about nine in 1960. Mine was brown, black and yellow tartan and very chic.

Under the watchful eyes of Mrs Darbishire

But patchwork and quilting only arrived in my experience when I reached secondary school. We had a lovely, gentle, elderly (to my innocent eyes) lady who taught us to sew. Mostly, she let me get on with whatever I was making. After all, I could lay out a pattern, pin it, cut it out, tack it and sew it. I had already learned that at home. It was a joy to spread out a crisp new tissue paper pattern on a group of tables, when I had only been used to laying out on the floor before.

The refinements of needlework, I learned from Mrs Darbishire; tailor's tacks, French seams, using pinking shears, arrow-headed pleats, invisible mending and invisible patching, embroidery, hat steaming and blocking..... and on the occasions when one of us had finished an item, or had forgotten to bring our sewing, we worked on English paper pieced patchwork.

Sewing with friends

I remember sewing with a friend, skinny as a lath, who made a circular mini skirt which looked sensational. I tried so many times to emulate it but never could. I just did not have the hips for it.

I sewed with a classmate, who made an evening dress in purple crepe. It had an empire line and tiny pin tucks, and was edged with lace. I could not understand why she did not make the lovely Victorian pin-tucks. Until she quietly disappeared from the class and we eventually learned that our golden youth was not forever. She had died of cancer at 17.

I remember making a striped smock and getting away with using it as my school summer uniform. I also made a wraparound skirt in navy, and, yes indeed, wore it in the winter.

I loved sewing, but hated patchwork

Cutting up fabric from the laden stalls at our local market to make the latest fashion was great: cutting up fabric to sew together in tiny bits just didn't make sense; it was old fashioned.

Really, what was the point of patchwork? After all, it wasn't wearable! I wouldn't be going out in it at the weekend, would I? In short, at this time, I loved sewing, but I hated patchwork.

Inspired by mum, yet again

But, like my peers, I did do patchwork - as rarely as I could. Cutting papers, cutting fabric leftovers from the scraps of 500 girls, sewing, tacking and stitching the hexagons took time, and, at the end of it, you had a few square inches of patchwork. And, apart from a pathetic attempt at Liberty lawn clamshell patchwork in the nostalgic 70s, that was it for me. Until now, and all thanks to my mum.

My mum moved on once her brood had fledged. She retired and took classes in floristry, lampshades and patchwork; and she fell in love with hexies and hand quilting. She made quilts for us all, and my spare bed still sports a blue and orange log cabin quilt she made. A lovely Trip Round the World, which she pieced, but gave me to finish, is my cuddle quilt. As I look at it, I reminisce over the patches of my kids' toddler clothes, my maternity nightie, my daughter's little dresses, my Laura Ashley curtains from the 80s. Memories, hopes and happiness. It set me off again...

Sewing to control a hurricane

Towards the end of her life, mum moved into a sheltered flat and found a little group of sewing friends. They made and raffled quilts for charity to the tune of thousands of pounds. I, in turn, retired, and fell in love with speed piecing and free motion quilting. My sewing room now is a riot of frivolity, scraps of leather, felt, silk, organza and piles of fat quarters.

Now it is my turn, as I have granddaughters, one of whom, aged three, has seen me produce princess dresses and dress her dolls in an afternoon. She has hair the colour of marmalade and a temper to match - sunshine with a dash of hurricane. She is rarely still and never quiet. Yet she sat silently on my sewing room floor while I fashioned fleece cloaks for her two dolls.

I have happy memories. And I have high hopes...

This is identical to the machine for my first lessons in sewing

A starter but not a finisher

By Juliet Nice

I've always sewn, always crafted. You name it, I've tried it. My first venture into quilting though, was in my early teens - a kit with plastic hexagon templates. I had no patience for hand sewing so that was short lived and swiftly forgotten. A few years later, I stayed at a friend's house and her mum hand-sewed quilts - start to finish, all by hand. She sold them for about £500 (which is about £1500 today). I was never going to hand-sew one but they were so beautiful they stuck in my mind. I still have the occasional go at hexies, which inevitably end up in a drawer after I've made a few and then quit.

My first quilt, my first finish

My first quilt ended up being a baby quilt for my firstborn, though of course not actually finished before he was born, that would be silly! I didn't have a book or anything; I just drew on my general sewing knowledge and went for it. It was mostly cotton but where I couldn't find the right colour it was polycotton, as was the backing. I drew around a cardboard square and cut out with scissors, and then sewed every square with a matching colour thread. My favourite bit now is the quilting; stitch in the ditch with matching thread and the teeniest-weeniest short stitches - what was I thinking? I do like to hold it up as a testament to polycotton, having been washed at 60° and 100° multiple times it's faded but still going. But I did finish it and it's had plenty of use over the years.

My sewing machine gathered dust

It would be another decade before I picked up quilting again. I always had a sewing machine set up wherever I lived but it never got much use. I left home at 17 so between work, going back to college and then marriage, babies and divorce, crafting had taken a back seat. One day I discovered rotary cutters on a TV shopping channel, and with a kit from them too, I finally sat down at my sewing machine again. Not that I finished much, which has become my usual! Over the following years I quilted but sparsely, up to the day I found a quilting group on Facebook and started UK Quilters United.

That was the beginning of all of this and five years later there is so much to UKQU that it's a full-time job to keep up with it all! It's become one of the most important things I've ever done and I'm so proud of it all.

It sent me on a path where my lounge is now my sewing room and everything I need is readily available so that I can sew whenever I want. My latest addition is a quilting frame, though no machine to go with it yet. One day! Depression makes me less than enthusiastic most of the time, but now I'm ready to go whenever I get that spark.

Still not a finisher…

I'm not saying I spend a lot of time quilting now, but I do spend a considerable amount of time thinking about it and watching over UK Quilters United and ukqu.co.uk, and buying fabric, of course. But if I start something, I rarely finish it.

So, while everything has changed, some things never will.

Find me online at ukqu.co.uk/members/juliet/blog

Nobody puts baby in the corner…

By Christine Hutchins

I was never the first to finish when it came to craft projects in school. I remember a piece of weaving we did and it seemed that I was always behind – I didn't manage to make as much in the session as other pupils did. I put this down to me being a bit particular about the yarns I was using – they were fine (not chunky), and I also wanted one yarn per row. This should have been a bit of an indication for other crafting activities throughout my life.

Slightly before this, I recollect tearing up small pieces of shiny paper to use as a mosaic on a bell cut-out, so that we could use glue to stick the pieces to the shape we had chosen. I had interpreted the design brief (at five years old, it must have had another name) a little more literally – with small pieces of shiny paper, and so it took ages to tear the pieces and then stick them down. As it took so long, I was encouraged to use bigger pieces (which I didn't really want to do), and it could easily be that someone else finished it for me (we were doing it as a Christmas activity, and I didn't get to be in our reception class nativity play, because I had a hospital appointment that day – a follow up to the operation I had had that summer for grommets). At the end of it all, I had a completed piece – but, even though 39 years have passed, it was never the piece I intended it to be – possibly because I was forced to complete it in a way that I did not want to.

Rush, rush, rush; finish it quickly

In school we were encouraged to finish things quickly – that a judgement was made if you were one of the last people to finish. I had a similar issue later in my primary school, when we made a towelling beach bag with a plastic lining and our initials embroidered on it – I well remember having quite a problem with chain stitch.

The towelling beach bag

This had not been my first foray into the world of embroidery – we had done some in year two (which we called third year), when we made a Binca mat with simple embroidery.

Starting young

I watched my mum knit, sew, crochet and make rugs. I was delighted when she gave me some hexagons, and I set to sewing them together – without using templates.

Around this time, my dad made me a sewing box – like the one he had made my mum. I still have it, and I have the needle case my mum made for me too.

A little later still, when I was around ten years old, I acquired some hexagon templates, and started my little project again. A friend of mine was doing the same, and we often got together to sit and stitch. She always seemed to finish her projects first, although on closer inspection, she did not use as many stitches along the edge as I did…

When it came to sports, I was one of the last to be chosen, and even when it came to crafts, I was not really in a league with others in my class. At that time, I was more interested in my flute lessons than in doing the lessons in school, as I knew that I could hone my craft skills at home.

Needle case and sewing box, made by mum and dad respectively

Friday night in

Friday evenings I remember with affection; I was not one to go out to clubs – I was not on a bus route, and it took me some time to learn how to drive. I was out for other evenings during the week, and so Friday night was a night in.

We sat in front of the television – enjoying such delights as Dynasty, The Cosby's, Gardener's World, and Love Hurts (Adam Faith and Zoe Wannamaker – how I loved that series!). Sitting watching these programmes was a chance for me to sit and do my patchwork – a real joy.

Patchwork comes to university

In 1993 I went to university, and I took my patchwork with me. I was a little embarrassed to bring it out at first, as I viewed my much-loved hobby as being a bit old-fashioned, and was not certain how others would view my 'strange' hobby. I needn't have feared, as my work was admired – and for only the second time, it seemed that I was somebody – I was a fish in a pond – not just a tadpole! The cleaners of our hall saw me sewing, and gave me one of the sheets, so that I could use it to back the quilt I was making.

I continued sewing with hexagons, and having planned out a Grandmother's Flower Garden-style quilt using isometric paper, I then started designing another quilt, this time using squares.

My first quilt

Moving for work

I moved to Devon to take up a new job. I was the baby in the department; I was by far the youngest. Even in years that followed in my first teaching position, when four or five other teachers joined our department, I was still the youngest. When I moved to a new school, and became Head of Department I was still the baby – the youngest – at 30 years old.

Here I was, Head of Department, the youngest of them, and I was not in the corner. I was the one making decisions, and trying to get others to embrace the change, embrace the new technology, try a new way of doing things.

Always the baby…

Once I finished there, I started a local quilting group; as there were none in my area. Once again, I was the baby. This also seemed to be the case when I attended workshops at my local quilt shop; I was the youngest.

At the workshops, a change was taking place – I may not have been the first to finish – although I can remember one workshop where I was, but I was not the last either. The difference was that once I got home, I was able – and inspired – to get on and finish the project (the top at the very least), and I was fully convinced of my ability to complete the project.

Soon after leaving my teaching position, I attended a local quilt show; this was a great experience, and I joined the quilt group. Once again, I was the baby of the group; this wasn't much of a surprise, as the group meets on a Wednesday morning, and there are not many women in their mid 40's who are able to attend weekday groups.

... but definitely not in the corner

However, although I am still the baby of the group some seven years later, I am also asked for my opinion. I have been sewing/quilting for longer than some of our members, and I am certainly one of the loudest (being a teacher has its advantages sometimes – it means I can make myself heard).

I have over 30 years of sewing experience, and being left-handed, I can help others who are also left-handed; I can help them when they find some of the instructions rather confusing or difficult to follow.

Sewing, quilting, embroidery, crafting – this is my life – and I have finally found my place in it. I am in my element – and able to share my experience with others. It has taken me many years to find my place, and to accept and realise that I do not have to be one of the first to finish; being first can be a good experience and can be rewarding.

However – finishing something to the best of my ability, making it the way I want it made, and in my own time, recognising that this is the way I need to work, is more important and more rewarding than finishing something first. I'm still the baby of the group – but my work and expertise mean that I am never in the corner any more.

Find me online at christine-quiltingatwestdene.blogspot.com

Choosing what *I* keep from quilting magazines

By Linda Lane Thornton

If you were restricted on space and weight when travelling (or living onboard a boat, like I do) and thus had to choose what to keep each time you receive a quilting magazine – what articles or features would you keep?

For a number of years my copies of a particular quilting journal have been sent to my brother's house in South Africa. I visit him at least once a year, so I go from famine to feast with regard to quilting magazines and journals. Unfortunately, I visit him by air, so I have to be careful of excess baggage. While in South Africa I also take the opportunity, to stock up on such delicacies as Marmite, unobtainable where I now live in the Azores, but essential to my darling husband. This means I have to look through the journals and magazines and take out to bring with me only what I want to keep as a reference.

My favourite content of quilting magazines

My latest sojourn with my brother revealed something of which I had been only vaguely conscious: - there wasn't a single patchwork or quilting pattern in what I had saved. What I had torn out to keep were:

- three items about textiles from other parts of the world
- two items about North Country wholecloth quilts
- two features about Welsh quilting
- one about a specific piece of corded quilting
- one about sashiko in Japan
- one about fidget (or fiddle) quilts and their benefits to those coping with dementia
- one about a group of quilters in early 20th century County Durham.

But, what about quilting patterns?

My selection gave me cause to think about what aspects of quilting and patchwork I like and how I spend my precious time. Often, I will see a pattern – on the internet, in an advertisement or a feature article – and wonder how it is constructed. Half-an-hour or so with graph paper, pencil, eraser and rule and I have usually managed to draft the pattern. However, I've no intention of actually turning these patterns into quilts or wall hangings. I have two antique wholecloth quilts and four patchwork quilts at home, so the exercise is more a question of draughtsmanship and geometry, than that of pattern-draughting; it's fun and gives my brain a quick gymnastic workout.

The flowing, graceful, delicate patterns to be found on wholecloth quilts are an endless source of fascination and one day – this mythical day in the future when I have nothing else to do – I will draft them out so that they can join the other wholecloth quilt patterns in my collection.

Bring me stories and quilting techniques

I have realised that I like features that I want to READ; items which will either add to the databank that I call my brain, or will give me a new perspective on a theme. I enjoy items about techniques too, e.g. prairie points, reverse appliqué, Japanese folded patchwork or kantha. Yes, it's lovely to see other quilts and to see the patterns, but I've got enough quilt patterns stored away in folders to last me a good few years. Nor do I want to clutter my limited space with too many gadgets.

I read about people having this or that, but I wonder if quilting gadgets are like kitchen gadgets: used a few times then left to gather dust. No, I haven't got much by way of gadgetry but it doesn't stop me making quilts or enjoying the benefits of having such a creative and rewarding passion.

Special friends

By Lyn Butler

Twenty years ago, we retired relatively early and moved to the West Country for the 'Good Life'. This wasn't an easy decision, leaving family behind, but our daughters were settled into relationships and we took the plunge. We settled in well and soon met our lovely new neighbours, Marie and Roger, who were soon to be our great friends. We were invited over one evening to meet their 'friends'...

'Come over about 10pm.'

10pm? A bit late we thought, as we're usually in bed by then!

Nevertheless, we popped over to their beautiful thatched cottage at 10pm and were invited into the kitchen. To our great surprise the lights were all out! We were asked to sit by the big window and look out onto their lit-up, immaculately lawned garden and then...one by one...the 'friends' started to appear.... BADGERS!

Marie told us that every night they came for their supper, brocks and cubs alike would feast on nightly supply of peanuts. What a wonderful sight!

Badgers, then patchwork

After a short while Marie introduced me to patchwork...that was just the beginning of an amazing journey!

I was really impressed with the lovely teddy bear quilt she made for her grandson.

To be totally honest, at first, I wasn't too sure about the thought of doing patchwork, but I didn't want to appear unsociable, so I gave it a whirl...a decision I've never regretted to this day.

Well, as many of you can relate, I became totally hooked. We spent many hours sewing together and shared many laughs and tears. Fortunately, our hubbies got on really well, they were both great DIYers; we affectionately nicknamed them 'Bodgit' and 'Scarper'.

Teddy bear quilt made by Marie

Over the next few years we spent some great holidays together, and I continued to get lots of support and encouragement from Marie in my patchwork projects and sewing activities.

Tearful farewell

I fast forward a few years, as we realised how much we were missing the family living so far away. We decided to move back, just in time for the grandchildren to start appearing... more opportunities for making quilts!

The moving day came and as we rolled out of our dirt track lane, the tears flowed when we waved goodbye to our wonderful friends. It was hard leaving, but we reminded ourselves that we were moving closer to our family.

We obviously kept in touch over the coming years, but sadly Marie became very ill and they decided to move to be near their family.

We kept in touch daily by messaging, as it was too painful for her to talk. She was struggling to do any patchwork, so for Christmas I bought her a book of felt animal patterns which she loved! She set to, making of course, her 'friend' the badger.

Making together despite distance

Now it was my turn to encourage and support her, so I kept her company by making her the 'cuddle' cat and we messaged photos to each other with our progress. Sadly, things got worse for my lovely friend and on our last visit, after a very emotional goodbye, her hubby handed me a bag and asked if I could take it and finish it for her. I was so delighted to finish off the badger 'friend' and thought about all the good times we had shared. When it was finished, I posted it off to her with the 'cuddle' cat.

Sadly, the post was delayed...it was too late!

Thank you to Marie

Marie was an amazing lady and she became a very good friend, who also encouraged and guided me when I learnt a new skill. She was generous in life and very brave in her illness.

As I now look back, I am left with wonderful memories of our special patchwork journey and friendship and I know she'll be up there teaching the angels to patch the clouds.

Find me online at ukqu.co.uk/members/lynb/blog

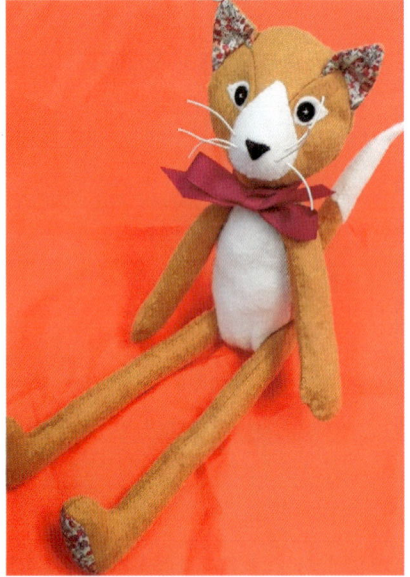

The badger and the cat Marie and I made

The Beginning

By Antonella M Jones

The beginning, September

Evie and Emm were sitting across from each other at Evie's kitchen table, a pot of fresh coffee between them.

"Well, what do you think then?" asked Emm of her friend.

Evie and Emm had become good friends through their sons, who were the same age and played together in the street in front of their houses.

"I'm not sure," replied Evie. "I've never stitched a thing in my life and now you want me to sign up for something I've never even heard of!"

Emm had come up with the idea of going to the local college for evening classes a few years ago, but they had so far stuck to what they knew best and had done a variety of cookery classes.

"I mean to say, American Patchwork for heavens sake, how did you come up with that one?"

Emm's mum had always sewn and knitted and Emm could knit any pattern she came across. Not so Evie, who would have been hard pressed to find a needle and thread in her mother's house – no crafty genes there!

"It'll be a change for us," said Emm, "and it's only for ten weeks. By then we'll know if we love it or hate it."

"OK, even I can manage one evening a week for ten weeks, You've talked me into it," replied Evie with some trepidation.

The first lesson

The following evening, a chill in the autumn air and a steady rain falling, Evie and Emm set off to the local college to sign up for the American Patchwork course and to collect the list of requirements. This was all very new to Evie, but the tutor seemed like a very nice lady, not at all like the home economics teacher she'd had in high school – that one would have fitted in very well at Hogwarts!

Evie was quietly excited and a little nervous the next week as she waited for the class to begin. She found the supplies list not too daunting, but who would have guessed that there were so many different types of needles! Fabric was something of a problem, as she didn't know yet what they would be making. She would just have to wait until next week to start the sewing, but somehow couldn't imagine that waiting would be a problem!

"Are you ready for this exciting new experience then?" asked Emm when she called in on Evie the day of their first class. "I wonder if we'll know anyone else there? The tutor runs a few of the same classes, so it must be fairly interesting."

"I think I'll be able to last the ten weeks," said Evie into her coffee cup. "Then it'll be back to cookery classes, or I may just take up flower arranging!"

Taking a deep breath, Evie asked, "I've seen those old quilts made up of hundreds and hundreds of little hexagons. Please tell me that we won't be doing those?"

"No," replied Emm, "I think that's called English patchwork and we're going to do American patchwork. There must be a difference."

That evening Emm picked Evie up. The college wasn't far and it was a clear night. Off they went, supplies at the ready.

They soon located the designated classroom and found they were joining a small group, just ten ladies and the tutor. Evie didn't know anyone there, which she found surprising, as it was a small town and she had lived there all her life, but they were a friendly bunch and were soon introducing themselves and chatting as though they'd known each other for years.

The tutor began by explaining the difference between English patchwork, which is sewn over papers, and American patchwork, which is sewn using templates. It was all Double Dutch to Evie, but she was a quick learner and soon began to make sense of it all. They were to begin by making a cushion and were introduced to templates and how to make them - so that's what the breakfast cereal boxes were for!

Checking out the patterns and making the templates kept Evie and Emm busy for the rest of the class and they were amazed at how quickly the time had passed. Even more of a surprise was how much Evie had enjoyed the whole evening and was even getting excited at the prospect of going to choose the fabrics for her cushion.

"So, what did you think?" asked Emm on the way home. She wasn't really sure if her friend was just putting on a brave face in front of all those strangers.

"Well, I can see myself enjoying this class," replied Evie. "But we'd better wait and see how I get on with the hand sewing next week. Maybe that will be my downfall."

For the next week Evie busied herself with running the family home, the usual cleaning, laundry and shopping taking up much of her time. This was why she loved these college evening classes. They took her out of her usual routine and gave her some 'me time', along with the chance for some adult conversation with people she probably wouldn't have the chance to meet during the usual round of school and after-school activities.

She managed a run to the fabric store while the children were in school and chose the fabrics for her cushion. She was secretly looking forward to the creativity of how she was going to place the colours, but was still nervous about those stitches!

The excitement of week 2

It was Evie's turn to drive the following week and she was at Emm's house with time to spare.

"I never thought I'd see the day when you would be early to go to a sewing class," said Emm, smiling proudly at her friend.

"Well, thanks to you, I'm trying something new and I can even say that I am enjoying doing something that never was on my agenda!"

When Evie and Emm walked into the classroom the second week, they were greeted like old friends and soon settled down to mark the fabric and cut out the shapes.

"OK, I'm ready to begin," said Evie to the tutor. She seemed to be awash with shapes of various sizes and colours, and was at a loss as to what to do with them.

Luckily, the tutor was a patient lady and helped Evie sort the muddle into something that resembled the top of the cushion she was setting out to make.

"Just use a small running stitch and you can even begin with a knot," she said. "Stitch along the lines you've drawn and you won't have a problem."

Evie couldn't believe the simplicity of the instructions, but sure enough, by the end of the evening half of the block was sewn together and it was looking pretty good too! How could it be time to leave already? Two hours went by really quickly when you were enjoying yourself.

This time, when Evie dropped Emm at her garden gate she asked her friend if there would be another course after this one, as she felt she still had so much to learn she couldn't possibly pick it all up in ten weeks! Emm was lost for words, never thinking that Evie would take to sewing like a duck takes to water. She had obviously found something that had brought out her artistic nature and was loving the whole experience and the people she had met, who all now had something in common.

Evie didn't think for one minute that she would be able to leave the rest of the stitching until the following class. The next day, as soon as the children were settled in school, the beds made and the dishes done, out came her sewing bag. Evie would never have guessed how relaxed she would feel sewing those small pieces of fabric together and the satisfaction she would get from finding that her colour placements were very good indeed. She was going to have to face facts here; it was beginning to look like she was hooked!!

Going alone, January

"You aren't going to like this," said Emm, as she and Evie were walking to the nearby school to collect their boys. Winter had set in and it was a cold, crisp day, the kind of day that calls for scarves and gloves, but the sun was shining and it was a pleasure to be out walking.

"I've decided not to continue with the patchwork classes – it's just not for me," said Emm.

Evie was taken aback at her friends' announcement; she was loving every creative minute and had thought that Emm was too.

"I like all the friends we've made, but I just can't see what I'm going to do with any more of the stuff we make," continued Emm.

Emm's house was tidy in the extreme; anything that didn't have a use was out. Not at all like Evie's; she couldn't bear to part with anything that might come in useful! Organised clutter was how Evie would describe it, but her family thrived on it, and maybe that was some of the attraction to this new patchwork hobby, trying to create order out of chaos!

The problem facing Evie was her lack of confidence; she had trouble going places on her own and conversing with strangers.

"But these people aren't strangers any more, they've become friends" assured Emm when Evie voiced her fears. "You really have an eye for colour and you've made some lovely things."

"Not to mention that I've even managed the hand sewing. I never dreamed that all these things could be achieved using just a little running stitch," laughed Evie, remembering how afraid she'd been to start those first stitches!

"I thought it was only fair to let you know," said Emm. "It'll give you some time to think about whether or not you want to go back on your own or if you want to try some other class."

There wasn't a doubt in Evie's mind. She knew that she wouldn't be going to any of the other classes on offer now. She was hooked after all! She would just have to pluck up her courage and go back on her own. As Emm had pointed out, these people had become her friends and once she'd started chatting, she'd forgotten her self-consciousness. The women were from different walks of life and of different ages, but that didn't seem to matter once they all sat around stitching and talking. They had something in common now and Evie found herself helping with colour choices and was amazed at her new found confidence.

Starting the Sampler Quilt

At the second session of the new term, the teacher said that they could begin making blocks towards a sampler quilt; this, Evie discovered, was a quilt made up of blocks of different designs and she was eager to start something new and different.

"Okay, that's decided then," Evie told herself in the bathroom mirror that evening. "I am going back to the class on my own. I really want to make this quilt."

Evie was now on first name terms with her teacher, Rachel, and was soaking up all the knowledge that she could, both when Rachel was advising her or when she was giving advise or instruction to one of the other ladies.

She was especially enjoying playing with the colours and patterns of the fabrics and there seemed to be no end to the choices available. So far, Evie had completed two cushions, a table runner and a small wall-hanging, and she was extremely pleased with the finished articles. She had given the cushions to her Mum, who had given them pride of place and allowed no-one to sit on them!

Moving on, March

Just last week Evie had travelled further afield to a larger quilt store that had more fabrics than she ever knew existed! Two of the other ladies from the class, friends now, Suzie and Diana, had joined her on her excursion. It was a real treat to have a day out like this with friends. Spring was on the way and snowdrops danced in the breeze along the roadside. There was lots of laughter, stops for coffee and lunch, and plenty of time to savour the colourful array of fabrics at the quilt store. Not to mention all the notions, books and threads. The most difficult part of the day was deciding which fabrics to use for her Sampler Quilt.

"If you choose a focus fabric first," advised the assistant, "then you can pick out colours from that to either tone in or 'pop-out'."

This seemed to make some sense to Evie, so she concentrated on finding a fabric with a pattern and colours that she would enjoy working with. The fabrics were arranged around the store in colour collections and were as tempting as candy in the candy store. She avoided stripes and checks, as she didn't feel experienced enough yet to be able to place them accurately. She also avoided the really dark fabrics as she worried that she wouldn't be able to see the template lines that she had to mark. This still left hundreds of bolts of fabric of every colour imaginable to choose from. Eventually she chose a range in soft pinks and greens, and a white-on-white print for the background which she felt would add some texture without distracting from the block pattern.

It was a wonderful feeling, carrying that bag of fabrics home, a real achievement. She had made a start on her Sampler Quilt and could barely contain her excitement. She was now eagerly looking forward to the next class when she would begin marking the fabrics and cutting out the pieces for her blocks.

"Don't forget, accuracy is extremely important," reminded Rachel as the class started on their first block, "and patience helps too!" They were to begin with simple pieced blocks and work their way through to the more difficult ones, ones with set-in seams or curved piecing.

"Best not to think about those yet," thought Evie. "Just take one step at a time."

Today's block was the Churn Dash which consisted of basic squares and triangles and really wasn't a challenge to the class at all. However, it was to be the first of thirty blocks and Evie knew that some of the future ones would be a test of her ever-growing skills.

Catching the bug

Evie had taken to bringing her sewing out to work on in the evenings, once the children were safely bathed and tucked up in bed. The simple action of hand sewing was such a relaxing way to end the day and, as an added bonus, she had something beautiful to show for her efforts.

Evie's mother was amazed at her daughter's ability, but could not understand how Evie could be excited by hand stitching. Mind you, a few months ago Evie herself would have been amazed too. To think that she would be getting so much pleasure and a growing sense of achievement from the simple act of choosing fabrics, cutting them up, then sewing them back together again! Order out of chaos; something she was used to!

"Emm called round for coffee this morning," Evie said to Suzie and Diana – they shared a table each week now and helped and advised each other along the way. "She couldn't believe that I'm actually going to make a quilt, even though that was my reason for coming back to the class. I think she doubted my determination, but she did like the colours and fabrics that I've chosen."

"Well, we're glad that you came back. We all get along so well together that we've become a little group," said Diana. "We would really miss anyone who left now."

The sewing class and the friends she had met there had become the highlight of Evie's week and she was beginning to wonder how she had ever got along without it. This was something special in her life, something which gave her a growing self-confidence and her own identity.

"Block one is completed," Evie announced at the following week's class. There had been a couple of afternoons of cold rainy weather, which were ideal for sitting in front of a crackling log fire sewing. "I'd like to take a couple of block patterns home this week, just in case we have more bad weather".

"Wow!" exclaimed Suzie. "Who's going to be teacher's pet around here?"

Suzie worked full time and had to squeeze her sewing time into her lunch breaks and evenings, but she managed well and, being quite competitive, was eager to keep up with Evie.

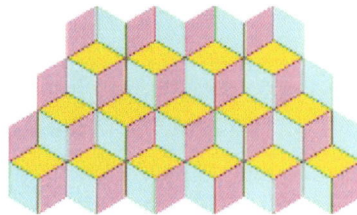

"I'm going to have to sew in my sleep, if you keep up this rate!" added Suzie.

This was the friendly banter that Evie loved; it was tossed back and forth across the table all evening with never a cross or sarcastic word among them, each woman praising another for some small achievement made along the way.

"Yes," thought Evie as she looked around the room, taking in all the now-familiar faces. Behind some of them was an ache of some kind, whether it was physical pain from illness or mental anguish at events in their lives, all was forgotten when they walked through the classroom door and Evie felt privileged to call them her friends.

"This is what has been missing from my life and now that I've found it, I'm here to stay."

Evie was sitting in her garden, the sun was shining and it was a warm day at the beginning of summer, there was a slight breeze, which was catching the edges of the fabric pieces she had laid out waiting to be sewn together. This was to be the final block of her sampler quilt. She had come a long way since that first class the previous September and looking back as she sewed brought a smile to her face. She had been so frightened about starting something new and now here she was, with twenty-nine different blocks waiting for this last one to complete her quilt. She had learned so many different techniques along the way, enjoying each and every one of them, and now sewed at home as often as possible as well as at the two-hour class where she met up with the rest of the group.

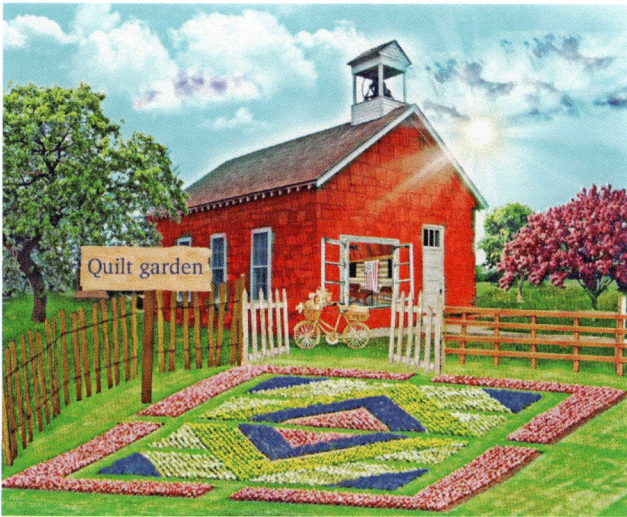

Planning for the Quilt Show, June

She had been on a few day trips with Diana and Suzie, seeking out quilt shops, with each of them looking out for one they hadn't visited before. Their fabric stashes were definitely growing, but they had yet to visit a quilt show. That was about to change! Evie had seen an advertisement in a quilt magazine for one to be held at a community centre a couple of hours' drive away.

"Do you fancy a day out, girls?" Evie asked Diana and Suzie the following day. They were having coffee in a little café in town on one of their regular Friday meetings, Suzie grabbing a bite to eat, as it was her lunch break too.

"I'd like to go to this quilt show, but don't fancy going on my own and my family won't want to go with me!"

"Maybe we'll find something new and exciting that we can start when we've finished our sampler quilts," replied Suzie. "I'm up for it. How about you Diana?"

"Just try leaving me behind," laughed Diana. "In fact, I'll drive, then I know I'll be going!"

"Wow, serious stuff," laughed Evie. "Now I'm really looking forward to it. I'd better start saving some money, there's sure to be lots of stuff I'll want to buy!"

At the next class Evie told the rest of the group about the up-coming quilt show and a few more ladies decided to go too. A couple of cars would be making the trip. The group arranged to meet up for lunch at the show, when they could tell one another of fabric bargains or special quilts they had come across.

Finishing the sampler quilt

In the weeks running up to the quilt show, Evie sewed and sewed. The blocks for her quilt were all made, so now she had to lay them out to find a pleasing overall design. She then put a narrow sashing between the blocks to give them a background. During the time she was sewing, she was aware that she was going to have to begin something new when she finished this and was hoping that she would find something that would excite her at the quilt show. In the meantime, her sampler quilt was coming together and was looking good. As she was becoming more experienced, she was beginning to realise that perhaps a change of colour here, or a different fabric there, would have been an improvement, but she was also sensible enough to know that she was on a learning curve, and that could only be a good thing. She was immensely proud of what she had achieved in such a relatively short time. Her friend Emm had been amazed when she saw the completed blocks mounting up and had told Evie how excited she was to think of the completed quilt.

Three weeks later Evie put in the final stitch and her quilt top was completed, all hand sewn, it was indeed a labour of love. She felt such a rush of pride and satisfaction as she looked at it; it represented a new beginning to Evie, a new hobby, new friends and a new-found confidence that went alongside being able to do something and do it well. It would be some time yet before the quilt was completely finished, it was still to be layered with batting and a backing, and then hand quilted, but she was going to enjoy it every step of the way. Quilting the blocks would bring new life to them, accentuating some sections and not others.

"What was your favourite block?" Emm had asked her last week. Evie had no answer for Evie, as each block had something to say. You could make even the plainest block sing, if you used the right colour and fabric combination, and that to Evie was what had drawn her into patchwork – a whole roomful of women could make the same quilt block and every one would be different. Individuality, that's what it is about, she thought. We are all individuals and so are quilts.

The day of the quilt show

The day of the quilt show came around quickly. The children had stayed at Grandma's overnight, so that Evie could be ready for an early start when Diana and Suzie called to pick her up. She was not a 'morning person', but today was different. Today she was going to her first quilt show and she was bubbling with excitement. They had decided not to stop for coffee on the way.

"We'll just get there, then have coffee before we hit the quilts and the vendors," proposed Suzie. "But I won't know where to look first," she continued.

"Should we have a plan of action?" asked Diana as they left. "Quilts then vendors, or vendors then quilts?"

"I think I would like to look at the quilts first," said Evie. "I'd like to see what other quilters are doing and to look at workmanship to see if I can gauge how well or how badly I'm doing. I might also get some ideas for a new project and will then be able to get the supplies from the vendors."

"Sounds like a plan to me," said Diana, "and quite a sensible one too considering how excited you are!"

Living in Yorkshire they were used to being surrounded by some of the most beautiful scenery in England, and today was no exception, driving across the wide expanse of rugged moorland and then through small villages where the cottage gardens were bursting with colour, reminded them how lucky they were to have all of this beauty just a few miles from home. The roses, which bloomed in so many of the gardens, had a soft-edged quality to them and had the car windows been open, Evie was certain that their perfume would be drifting on the breeze.

Nature threw so many colours and textures together and they all seemed to mingle perfectly. Surely, this was a lesson to anyone who worked with colour and pattern.

As they approached the hall where the quilt show was being held, they saw animated groups of ladies chatting excitedly as they made their way towards the entrance. Evie, Diana and Suzie soon became a part of the crowd waiting for the doors to open, and then they were inside!

Finding inspiration

Evie wandered around the large hall among quilts and wall hangings of different sizes and colour combinations, some she wouldn't have used herself and some that were a pleasant surprise when put together. Some of the quilts were poorly put together or quilted, but as one of the ladies from her class pointed out over lunch, we don't know the background of that quilter, maybe she has arthritic hands, or poor eyesight, but she's tried nonetheless. This gave Evie food for thought and she vowed not to be too judgmental in future.

Other quilts were amazing in the techniques and abilities on show and must have taken many months of painstaking work to complete. Evie didn't think that she would ever belong to that elite group of perfect quilters. She did love doing what she was doing, but she was always eager to begin the next project, and there was always something new just around the corner!

"I don't think I was born with a competitive gene," said Evie, as they gazed in awe at the prize-winning quilt.

"There is no way on earth that I could come up with such perfection. I'll just have to settle for the fact that my quilts will be used and loved, and the little imperfections are just a part of who I am!"

"Have you seen anything that you would like to do next?" asked Diana.

"I've chosen a Dresden Plate quilt for my next project. I can use up some of my fabric scraps for the 'plates', but I'll need to buy some neutral fabric for the backgrounds," responded Evie.

The story so far...

From those early days, 30+ years ago, my life has certainly changed! The children that brought us together are now happily married and have given us wonderful grandchildren, husbands have retired and our hair has greyed (well, not mine – I know a good hairdresser!).

I took the City and Guilds Part 1 at our local technical college. I became a patchwork and quilting tutor, passing on the craft to so many lovely ladies and setting them off on their own journeys. I even had a foray into owning my own quilt shop. I have travelled to quilt shows across Europe and America with friends from that very first class and new ones made along my journey.

Throughout all this time there has been a constant core of friends from those first classes and we have been through every aspect of life together, from the sad times when all you needed was a kind word and a hug, to the happy times when you needed someone to dance on the table with you! (Metaphorically speaking, of course!)

The life of a quilter is indeed like a patchwork quilt, made up of so many different pieces and stitched together with love.

I'm ready and waiting for the next chapter!

Finding support in quilting

Should I stay, or should I go

By Jane Galley

When a UKQU Bloggers' retreat was first announced I was thrilled at the idea. I'd never been on a retreat before and, as the excitement grew and everyone was discussing in the Facebook group what to take, I was at home sitting in fear and trepidation. I was thinking of how to back out of the retreat without causing upset or of course, feeling like I'd wasted the money I had paid towards it. Let me explain why.

On the outside, everything is fine

After the birth of my second child, I had postnatal depression. As part of that, my natural introversion became something much bigger. The front door became a big barrier to the outside world; where I didn't want to be. I was happy at home with my boys and, as they got older, I would have to force myself to go out for them. Over the years, the feeling of panic about going out lessened a bit, but it came back with a vengeance some years ago. For about three years, I didn't go out alone and at one stage I couldn't even go out of the back door to hang the washing.

Thankfully, that has passed and to anyone looking in, everything is ok. However, even though I have a fulltime job, every time I go out is planned to the most minute detail. I have my set places to park and know where my safe places are. It certainly gives me empathy when working with my students. When I see the panic in their eyes at unfamiliar situations, I'm right there with them. I help them develop their coping mechanisms, just as I've developed mine.

My crafting and quilting are my safe places, they help me to deal with having to go out in the real world where I have to meet and interact with people. They give me time to allow my brain and body to relax and I need regular doses of that to be able to continue doing what I do. This is where the mixed feelings with the retreat came in, so let's get back to the retreat.

Mixed feelings about going

As I wrote above, when the retreat was first announced, I thought it was a great idea. I would get to meet, in person the people whose blogs I read on the ukqu.co.uk website and speak to in the special Bloggers' Facebook group. We would have the opportunity to develop ideas together and get to know each other better and I thought it would be a great opportunity to be immersed in the quilting world for a weekend.

On the other hand, I was going to a place I didn't know, where I hadn't been able to plan my parking, and where I had no control over the room I would be in. Add to that, knowing that I would be meeting, face to face, 25 people I didn't even know virtually a year ago! I had this battle going on in my head telling me I'll be OK, we'll have a good time, but, the "What if???" was still lurking at the back of my head.

"Still, I knew, if I didn't go, I'd regret it."

Sometimes, writing down on paper how I feel, or in this case, typing it on the screen, as a blog for the website, helped to put it all into focus. I had thought the blog would disappear into cyberspace, and that would be it. However, it seemed to strike a chord with others in the group and they shared their own stories of struggles with me. This made me think, that perhaps it wouldn't be so daunting after all when I arrived for the weekend.

Taking control of the situation

I got to the retreat early, which meant I entered an almost empty sewing room and could strategically choose my position. I opted to sit right at the door, so I could see everyone in the room, and being right by the door meant that in case there was a need to escape, I could do so quickly (and quietly).

The sewing room was open late for the night owls and open again early in the morning for the early birds. It was fantastic being able to sew without worrying about getting meals or cleaning up for a whole weekend. I thoroughly enjoyed getting to know some of the other bloggers, gleaning lots of hints and tips along the way. It was well worth quashing the fear and doubts and getting myself there.

Doing it again, and trying something else new

This year, the retreat is being in held in the same venue, so now I know where I am going, where I can park and the routine for getting booked in and for meals.

I am doing something else for the first time in over twenty years; I am going to a quilt show; now that is a whole new basket of fat quarters!

Find me online at www.loopysplace.co.uk

The Bloggerati retreat goodie bag
(photo by Sylvia Priest)

Quilting to a song

By Denise Inkson

Music has always talked to me, from my earliest memory of standing up between the two front seats of my parent's car (those were the days before safety belt laws), singing my little heart out to inspiring the way I now think, feel, write and sew. We never truly have a quiet house except for when everyone but me is out. Music plays from every room. At one point, it became white noise to me. While the girls were growing up their songs competed for airtime and would drive me insane. Now they like similar songs and genres so they share the music; however, it has just gotten louder. My youngest loves music and can play the bass guitar, piano (keyboard) and melodica. The sound resonates through the floorboards, and I can hear it while I sew in the dining room. Not that it bothers me. I love hearing the learning process while I stitch away on my machine, even if the tempos of both do not match up.

Listening to music

Stepping back in time to when I was a child, listening to music in my aunt's car while traveling on holiday. My aunt loved country music and now I do too. I was enthralled by a Dolly Parton song, A Coat of Many Colours. It tells the story of a mum's struggle to clothe her children and how she had been donated a bag of rags, and with those rags she made a coat. To the child the coat was worth all the money in the world, because her mother had stitched the coat with love. As the mother stitched, she told the child the story of Joseph and his coat of many colours. The other children did not understand the story and only showed meanness and cruelty. They failed to realise that beauty lies more in things that are given with love, than in how much they cost to buy.

When I was little, money was scarce, and my mum, a single parent had to rely on my grandparents for food parcels each week to keep things going. My grandfather often re-purposed things for us to play with, for example washing line poles became stilts. These things were worth more to me than the genuine purchased ones, because they were made with love. So that song really inspired me, it has remained with me throughout my life.

Mirror into the past

Imagine the scene: a 16-year-old living in one bedroom, in another family's house with no one and nothing to call home. This was my reality coming from a children's home once I had finished my secondary education. It was considered a form of adult training designed to make 'me' ready for the real world. In my view it was a way of ticking those boxes - social services saying they were helping.

> I was a child from care; care that is an oxymoron as
> no one cares when you are in the system.

They had originally tried to place me with a lovely family, but I ended up falling for the son, so that was a no go. Instead, I was given a small box room within a family's home, at first, they were friendly but I now feel that they thought they were getting a live-in maid.

With no money and no opportunity to go to college, I worked on a YTS project (Youth Training Scheme) – I believe they refer to them as apprenticeships nowadays. I did mine in secretarial work and Computer Aided Design. I passed the YTS scheme with a distinction, not bad for me as my mother called me stupid growing up. Sadly, that statement has plagued me for most of my adult life.

Unfortunately, things did not work out with the family and my social worker found me a bedsit in a shared house. Not the best environment, for a 16-year-old girl; the other tenants at the time, were all older men. I made the best of it and made friends with a couple. Rent was £30 a week, wages were £30 a week and housing benefit was taking forever - that was also the year that a woman prime minster and government stopped a selection of benefits to help the under 25's.

To help me out, my then landlord offered me a job collecting glasses on a Friday, Saturday and Sunday night, this money just covered the food. It was hard and life was unforgiving.

My only crime was leaving my single mother to live with my father at the age of 12 and my mother never wanting me back when things broke down with my dad and his new family.

Home was not where the heart was

I met a boy and 'fell in love', at only 16–17 years old the world starts and ends with love, or the perception of it. I left my bedsit and moved towns to live with him. Things did not work out. I was emotionally insecure and he was attached to his mother's apron strings. I had to move out in a hurry as he had left to go back home and I was going to be homeless as the flats were only for couples. As an emergency, I moved into my cousin's house, until I discovered she was stealing from me and had to move from her fast - so fast, in fact the new landlady even helped collect my things. I moved back to my original town and into a different bedsit. This one was a shared house where the landlady and landlord lived on the premises. A cold one-bed room on the top floor of a three-storey building; the owners would sit and watch television in front of their fire while the rest of us froze. After a period of months, not sure how many, I moved yet again. To another bedsit, warmer, not warm but better. I swore to myself then I would never go cold again.

Undervalued and underpaid jobs

A few years later and different jobs, mainly in the undervalued and underpaid care sector of the elderly, some secretarial work, eighteen months in the Territorial Army as a medic, and one year in a school in what is now the role of a teaching assistant. I was stable for a while. At the age of 21, I moved to a new town, this is now the town of my home and the birthplace of my two daughters.

It was an educating time

I met my husband in 1995 and our first daughter was born in 1996. I was 23 years old and felt in so many things I had been there and done that and was lightyears away from being a naive young person. My husband, five years older than me, had already been in a marriage, and was slightly broken too. I was finally able to afford to go to college, but after I found out I was pregnant, I could no longer do that course – Travel and Tourism. It would have been hard to see the world with a baby in tow. I had wanted to stand on coaches and be that travel guide who would tell you about places, combining my love of history and travel.

Moving forward to 2001, with a surprise unplanned pregnancy while I was on the coil, we welcomed the birth of our second child. It was also around this time that I received the diagnosis of Fibromyalgia.

In 2007, our second child was diagnosed with Asperger's syndrome - an autistic spectrum condition; this was a life changer, we were finally getting answers, things made sense.

In 2008 I was working as a loans administrator and later debt collection manager for the Credit Union. To help my local Credit Union, I also enrolled on a foundation degree course in advertising and marketing to help the company as they could not afford to use an external marketing company. I was studying and working at the same time, juggling it all with busy family life.

Family and health first

Things then took a turn for the worse, when the government funding stopped for the Credit Unions all over the United Kingdom and both my roles ceased. At the same time my health and the needs of my children changed. I could no longer work 40 hours per week, as needed in marketing. In the second year at college I changed courses and started year one of the new course. I graduated in 2011 with a Bachelor of Arts in Professional Writing.

My husband, although a qualified electrician was in and out of work and most of our married life we have relied one way or another on benefits. It might have been better financially for us, had my husband wanted to work away, but leaving the family for him was not an option. When it did become an option for him, the costs of being away, outweighed the benefits. We have never been able to own our own home and due to poor decisions made in our youth, we have spent most of our life paying off debts. Money is something that never stays around long enough in our home to become savings.

Supportive and lovely friends

Life is not all bad, my husband and I are still married at the time of writing this in 2019; twenty-two years through thick and thin. Our friends have been angels, supportive, lovely and the best in the world. Our girls have had the basics - love, food, a stable roof over their heads, clothes, the best shoes, and even camping holidays. Although if you saw inside our tent it was more like "glamping" with a king size airbed and two singles, a portaloo, heaters, tent carpet and camping fridge. We even had a camping unit with a sink. Yes, we took the kitchen sink!

Mirror, Mirror, sew me a legacy

Move forward in time, to 2011, at 38 years old I was deeply dreading my 40th birthday. Added to that, this was the year the bedroom tax came into play. I feared what my future would be, actually I still do. All I could see was growing old in a cold bedsit all alone, the same way I had started my adult life. With no money and with nothing of value (materialistic wise) I was very depressed.

I was grieving leaving my degree and suicidal, as I stood looking in the mirror and seeing this nightmare become reality in front of my eyes, my thoughts turned to my girls, what legacy would I have to leave behind? What could they have that reminded them of me, all I had was a computer, few clothes and nothing much. The items in the loft from my nana and granddad would mean nothing to them, as we had no place to have them on display.

I loved sewing and had made small blankets, changing bags, as well as other items over the years. The one thing I had always wanted to make was a quilt. I had imagined sitting around talking to others and sewing together. Inspired by many television series such as The Walton's, Little House on the Prairie, Touched by an Angle - both old and new versions - as well as other films throughout the years. I started to look for groups or courses.

God was smiling on me as I found one! It was run by a lovely elderly and very knowledgeable woman called Sheila Butcher. This was a course for beginners so we were all setting off from the same place. We were all making the same quilt.

I had saved for months, trying to afford the fabric she said was required - a jellyroll. I had no idea what that was. I soon discovered it was fabric strips, 2½ inches wide, consisting of coordinating fabrics. I must confess, on top of the course, that the cost of the jellyroll at £45 was a bit of a shock. I had the money, as I had been prepared, but not knowing what a jellyroll was, when I saw it, the cost shocked me! Most of us were using the same fabric brand, and some even noticed that the strips bowed a little and were not cut properly. I had wondered why some of the blocks did not work, but being inexperienced I had no idea there was a reason, rather than my own inexperience. You would think at least they could be cut properly for £45. I have never touched that brand since for jellyroll packs.

My Sparkling Gemstones quilt

Creating Sparkling Gemstones

Sheila was teaching us how to make a jellyroll quilt named Sparkling Gemstones. It was enjoyable to make, although the hardest thing was matching the colours.

Sparking Gemstones (quilt size 58"x96"):
- Block size: 6"
- 9"x12" blocks & 2" wide boarders
- Large jelly roll of more than 40 strips or 40 strips of 2 ½" strips of assorted colours
- 63" of background fabric
- 20" of fabric for the boarder
- 20" of fabric for the binding

Sounds simple enough, right, but who knew that it would be so difficult!

Showing off the amazing backing fabric

The mysterious jellyroll, making the patches to make a quilt

The one thing about jellyrolls is the mystery behind the actual fabrics patterns and colours. You can see a certain colour theme, but not all of the choices in the pack are visible when purchased. Sometimes you can get one with all of the fabrics you like and sometimes you find about three or four different patterns and colours you do not. However, I consider this a quirk and can often add challenges to your normal pattern matching and add extra creative flare.

Week by week the quilt grew, blocks were made and rows added. As an added bonus, the friendships formed from the weekly sessions grew week by week too. We soon realised, that at our level of experience, only if you sew every day and really fast, could you have that quilt made within the course duration of six weeks,. The course was extended and we paid for the term. I was paying equally for the company of others, as I was for the learning experience. Except for school events or emergencies, the family knew no interruptions were allowed on Wednesday nights.

Learning two lessons

Time came to fit the wadding and backing. I needed the quilt to be machine washable and tumbled dried so I purchased wadding that would allow for that. As the quilt was for my eldest daughter, I thought it would be a good idea to include her in the edging and backing fabric choices. She selected a front edging in black with sheep on and for the back a pattern of colours resembling fireworks going off. With the fabric cut and brought to the till, the bombshell came in the form of the price. Apart from the jellyroll, all my fabric purchases up until this point had been under £8 per meter. The backing she had chosen was £13 per meter! I know, I should have checked the price, but this was an heirloom item and I wanted it to be what she liked and would enjoy. I paid the price and the first lesson learnt; check the price before the fabric is cut.

The second lesson I was to learn was in the use of it. So far, I had been working on cheaper priced material and I immediately noticed the difference when using better quality fabrics. Before now, I had not really considered this; but from then on, when I am choosing fabric, I factor in price, quality and usage. If I cannot afford it, I wait until I can and do not buy cheaper materials, as cheaper is cheap in the long term.

A quilt with a theme tune

When I make things now, that Dolly Parton song is in my heart and mind and I never sew angry or upset, I only wish to sew with love in my heart. That is what I did with my daughter, Deanna's quilt, made every stitch with love.

When the time came to give it to her, before she could have it, she had to listen to one song. Yes, I asked she listen to Dolly Parton's Coat of Many Colours. I knew she had listened to it, as she came to me in tears, then I handed her the quilt and we both shared love and a few more tears.

The quilt I made her is her pride and joy. I never knew how much until last year when she told me about her using it in a university lecture. The lecture focused on objects and their meaning to the owner.

Deanna took her quilt in and told them about it, she explained about the song and played it to the listening audience. According to her, most of them were in tears. When people asked to touch the quilt and feel it, she said "No!". No one can sit on it or touch it. Despite the fact that the quilt can be machine-washed and tumbled dried. It must only ever contain her smell and the smell of home.

Her story filled my heart with joy and my wish of an heirloom item was fulfilled.

A rag doll for my Kira

At the time of making the quilt for Deanna, I asked Kira, my youngest, if she wanted one too, but she said "No, thank you". She wanted a rag doll instead. Rosie was made from an old towel, with a self-drafted pattern. Kira was over the moon. At the time she would not really have understood the song, although she would have heard me playing it often at home. Instead, she had a homemade rag doll, which she loved. The irony being, when growing up, I had an old rag doll made by my late Nana.

Funny, how life can go full circle and it is not even the end; full circle, full joy.

Find me online at ukqu.co.uk/members/deedominix/blog

66

Quilting for pleasure and therapy

By Rebecca Nevard

I cannot remember a time when I didn't sew. From as far back as I can remember, I have known how to sew by hand and use a sewing machine. From cushions and curtains, to clothing and stuffed animals, I have always made something. As a teen, I vividly remember the summer after my GCSE's, going to Birmingham rag market and buying a mountain of fabric. I lovingly spent a whole summer making curtains, cushions and a bedspread for my childhood bedroom. Oh, such happy times, idyllic memories! To have eight whole weeks to sew, sew, sew and nothing else! Jump forward to my twenties and I was making home furnishings for my new home. Curtains, cushions, and even reupholstering an old sofa. Oh, how I loved my sewing machine.

"When I was a child, I spoke as a child, I
understood as a child, I thought as a child: but when I
became a (wo)man, I put away childish things."
1 Corinthians 13 verse 11

However, as my career blossomed and certainly, when I started to study for a degree in my spare time, sewing became less and less important. My poor machine was left neglected and at some point over that decade, I had given it away. I was too grown up for all that kind of nonsense, besides I was earning enough, I could buy new shiny things, rather than have to make them. "What did I want with handmade…."

Oh, how wrong I was. When I finally finished my degree, I was left with all this free time. I was itching to try something new, so I bought a new sewing machine, started reading up on quilting, and never looked back.

Image by Glesni Mair Wright

My version in fabric form

A seed was sown…. What pretty flowers!

I started small by making a few very basic jelly roll throws. When I say throws, they were not much bigger than cushions, but I loved it. A wife of a friend at work was pregnant with twins, so I offered to make them twin baby quilts; the scariest thing I had done to date. They were frankly really awful. My seam allowances were wonky and I used …. GASP <horror> …. polyester wadding. I know, the shame!!!! But I was still learning.

I paid for a day of one-to-one tuition with the amazingly lovely Shelagh Folgate. Oh my, it was like Blackpool illuminations, so many ideas!

I learnt about the joy of starching fabrics before cutting, and how wonderful non-polyester wadding is. If I was smitten with patchwork and quilting before, I was absolutely addicted then.

Moving house, far, far away

But then in my wisdom or insanity… I convinced my husband to move house; not just down the road, but over 200 miles, from Buckinghamshire to North Wales. What can I say; we were having our mid-life crisis!

When we moved to Wales, the deal was I would have my own sewing room. The only downside of moving to Wales is that work is scarce. I found work at a great company, but the drawback being it is 60 miles away. The drive is lovely (sometimes) and I get to wake up every day in the mountains. Since moving to Wales, quilting has become more than just a pleasurable past time or a hobby. It is now much more than that. It gives me time to unwind, relax and re-charge. Well…. when the pattern is easy to understand and you have not sewn that block wrong for the fifth flipping time!!!! AGGRH!!! And breathe……….

N.S.F.W. No sewing for weeks – blogging and more

I joined the UK Quilters United Facebook group not long after moving to Wales. Up until that point, I found quilting to be quite an anti-social and lonely pastime. I could lose hours <cough> days <cough> in my own little world singing along to music and sewing. However, moving to Wales, none of my friends lived nearby, so I very quickly came to rely on UKQU and other groups to be my social network. We laugh at each other's stories, we cry at other's misfortune, we share ups and downs. The other members are my surrogate big sisters, aunties and friends.

Late 2016 I was asked to join with a few of the UKQU community to start blogging for the newly formed website, ukqu.co.uk. I jumped at the chance. Roll on a year (and a bit) and despite my blogs petering out (work and lack of mojo getting in the way), and what a difference. I have attended my first retreat, written my first few patterns. I have not only participated in two mini quilt swaps, but also been a swap mumma (coordinator for the uninitiated). I have tried my hand on a mid-arm quilting machine and signed up to a local quilting group. I have made firm friends with a few and expanded my virtual social network massively.

But, what of the actual quilting… well, as life got in the way, and my mojo ebbed and flowed, the actual sewing seemed to dry up. I found more and more, I would rather be online talking to my friends than sew. My creativity and mood seem firmly linked.

Springtime - new growth and new plans

I am not sure about you, but I dislike all types of new year's resolutions. Who wants to make changes or plan for the future when all the glitz of the festive period is over and the weather is grim outside? All I want to do at that time of year is hibernate. It's hard enough getting the motivation to just function, let alone make sweeping changes to my life.

I think Spring is far more preferable as the time to make resolutions. Spring clean, out with the old, etc. I also find my mood significantly improves once the clocks changes and there is more sunshine in my life. Mojo restored and with a spring in my step, the thought of sewing is back! This is the year to be more mindful, and to plan for the times when the sewing mojo is not there.

Quilting as therapy

Just like in therapy, quilting can have many ups and downs. There are weeks where little progress is made and then sudden breakthroughs where a new technique is mastered. Like therapy, there are many different methods, but the end result is always a broken thing put back together in pleasing combinations.

Just like therapy, quilting is not for everyone, and just like therapy, we are always slightly ashamed of our own hard work, and yet proud and want to show of our progress without fear of judgement.

But, I say, be proud of your work. Be proud of every new skill learnt. Be especially proud of each and every quilt, finished or unfinished, no matter its flaws.

Every quilt is perfectly imperfect, exactly like every one of us.

Find me online at ukqu.co.uk/members/dotty/blog

The photo by Glesni Mair Wright, has been published with permission

Amongst these simple things

By a quilting friend

So another year begins and it brings a brand new start.
I only hope that quilting tends and heals this broken heart.

Winter numbs stitching fingers, sun and mood sink very low.
I miss my man so much now, seek him wherever I go.

March and the Beast from the East rages and roars round the land.
I hunt thimbles and match threads, take grief and sadness in hand.

Suddenly it's spring, cleaning, clearing the house, moving on.
Fabulous fabrics stay folded, my mojo has upped and gone.

Boxes and life all sealed up, will the bad days get much worse?
Books, stash and notions seem stuck, spellbound under grief's curse.

May welcomes in much missed light; our darling daughter is wed!
As toasts and speeches are made, so something shifts in my head.

Now the heat is oppressive, surely this cannot go on?
Summer time is here at last, so why hasn't my sun shone?

I find a place to call 'home', but don't know a soul down here.
Miss all the folks up country, really alone with my fear.

What to do? Just keep busy! Unpack the boxes and find...
My quilting, might it help me to regain some peace of mind?

What's this, deep in the quilt chest? Not just fabrics, but his shirts!
The lost ghost of his presence hits me so hard, how it hurts.

And this is where I find him, here, amongst these simple things.
At last I know what to do, the pattern's clear, my heart sings.

December and the work's done; I've found my peace, life is calm.
The memory quilt complete, keeps him close, we're safe from harm.

Patchwork & fabric addict plus an aspiring quilter

Gillian Griffiths

About 13 years ago, two days before Christmas I was diagnosed with breast cancer. I didn't tell my family until on 3rd January and I had a mastectomy the following day. Aggressive chemotherapy followed, then seven weeks of radiotherapy. I was not allowed to return to work as a school administrator, because of the risk of infection. I had several lymph nodes removed to ensure that the cancer had not spread, and this left me with lymphoma in my arm. This in turn allowed infection to take hold in my arm or hand on quite a regular basis. Each episode involved a four or five day stay in hospital whilst I received intravenous antibiotics. Eventually my GP put me on a daily dose of antibiotics which seems to have held infections at bay. I still have a mildly swollen arm and wear a compression sleeve and glove.

Time again, two years later

Then about two years later, over a weekend I felt a lump on the outside of my neck. It grew very quickly. My GP managed to get me an urgent hospital referral and I saw the consultant on the following Thursday. The lump was aspirated, then as the result of that I received a telephone call on the Friday. So it was back to the hospital. Cancer again... not related to my previous breast cancer. I spent Saturday morning in hospital having the offending material removed. Then followed seven weeks of radiotherapy, using the most grotesque net type mask. Another nine months off work.

Hitting a bad spot

I had by now changed schools, having worked hard to get a diploma for school business management. I loved my job, the children and colleagues. It was quite a stressful job, workload was heavy, there were leadership sickness and changes. But to shorten the story, I was very depressed, eating all the wrong things and gaining weight. I was home alone as my husband worked away during the week and my daughters were working and doing their own thing. I put on lots of weight - talking stones here - so ashamed now. But the depression was so bad I just didn't realise what was happening to me. I have since lost a lot of weight through determination.

Creating an addition

I had hobbies, including paper crafts and years ago dressmaking. After a particularly bad weekend coping with my feelings, my husband suggested trying something new, to channel my creative vibes. My grandmother showed me hexagon sewing many years previously so I looked up patchwork. I found a beginner's workshop with Jenny Lester at Midsomer Quilting, starting the very next day. They had a space available. My husband drove me there, five hours later an addict was released!

Learning about patchwork and quilting was a life saver, my brain was able to focus on something. I lost myself in colour and patterns; I felt better in myself whilst focusing on things not work related. I learnt so much in the first couple of years by taking hand and machine sewing lessons at a local retailer and travelling to Bramble Patch on Saturdays.

More challenges

Sadly, this progression didn't last. All the treatment I had gone through, together with ongoing medication caused many painful problems and the depression returned and I struggled at work. A change of management at the school created a very different working environment. I felt bullied, mistrusted - nothing was good enough - and there was no tolerance if I was having a physically bad day. I was also beginning to suffer from bad arthritis in my knees accompanied by pain, which added to the depression. Things came to a head when I turned up for a planned knee replacement and the surgeon refused to allow the operation to go ahead because of my health on the day. I was in so much pain, I completely went to pieces and could not return to face work problems.

Surprise quilt for my husband

Taking some time out

My GP agreed to sign me off work - I had one year off. During this time, I cried, and sewed, I could not go out, so I cried more. Then a friend called me and said there was a flower show nearby where quilts were also being shown and told me I was going to it! I went and I spoke to some lovely ladies who invited me to go along to their group meeting the following week. It was very hard, but another aspect to quilting was opened up to me. The group had quilters of all stages of experience, they had workshops, talks, competitions and advice by the bucket load.

I still felt far too unwell to return to work, anxiety and exhaustion made each day a challenge, but I could do a little sewing each day. Our eldest daughter had gone overseas to work and our younger daughter had had two little girls and a home with her partner. So, after much discussion my husband and I decided to downsize and move south, as we would be in a better financial place and perhaps I would feel better in a different environment. He still travels away to work, but I get by.

Sadly, anxiety still plagues me, along with deep seated pain. I have had, with great difficulty, to accept that I just cannot function and be reliable in employment. Standing is a nightmare, walking any distance is problematic and anxiety brings on asthma.

My first show and tell

Getting out every week

I live in a small village, so to get to know people I started a small quilting group. It was a very difficult decision, but it has helped me so much. I have to go out each week. I can now make decisions again. I have started to show other ladies how to sew. I also joined the Quilters Guild and by being on the regional committee have experienced different attitudes to quilting, and met quilters with different knowledge and interests. I live in the very south of our region, there is no one else nearby who attends events so it is a bit lonely.

Last year I even managed a visit to the Festival of Quilts, a fantastic array of quilts and all things quilting. Unfortunately, there was a problem with getting the booked disability scooter, which caused me a great deal of panic and anxiety, but I coped.

Day to day, I now accept my physical limitations and rest when my body tells me to. I manage by spending time sewing with beautiful fabric and keeping a very detailed appointment diary, because I get forgetful if under pressure! So, thank you patchwork for keeping me sane, now only to figure out how to master quilting! Which may drive me mad again!

Quilting as a therapeutic activity

By Jeanne Carlin

I have been sewing and quilting since I retired about six years ago. I use my quilting as a therapeutic activity, particularly at difficult times in my life. I have often heard other quilters say the same, so I thought I would use this chapter to explore what that really means to me .

Caring for my daughter

So, a bit about me – I have been a carer for my daughter, Erica for 36 years. She lived at home with us for 34 years and now lives in a residential home. She has multiple disabilities and a number of long-term health problems. She has seizures every day, she is fed via a gastrostomy tube over night and requires medication to keep her bowel working. Yet, saying that, she is a wonderful sociable woman who enjoys company and has a good life.

I have also over the past ten years supported my parents, initially to stay in their own home and later to move into residential care. My dad had dementia and died in 2013 and my mother has physical disabilities and long-term health conditions.

We are an immigrant family, so we do not have a lot of extended family around to offer support. At times, life can become rather stressful.

Sewing for therapeutic reasons

Although I sewed when I was younger and come from a family who have done dressmaking and tailoring for more than a century, I restarted sewing only just before I retired. I went to classes to learn both patchwork and quilting and also dressmaking.

I find I need to make space each week to do some sewing and I usually have a number of projects on the go.

So what need does this activity fill in my life? For me, my sewing fulfils three therapeutic purposes:

- it is a purposeful activity which distracts my mind and gives me a calm space;
- it raises my self-esteem and self-worth;
- it provides a new social network.

Finding distractions to cope

During 2015 and 2016 Erica became extremely unwell and she was at risk of her bowel perforating which would end her life. I turned to patchwork and tried to find as many opportunities each week to do some sewing. At the time of greatest stress, I opted to do a detailed log cabin design, which I found on Pinterest and titled 'Houses on the Hill'. The design and choosing colours for each house kept my mind busy and distracted me from dwelling on the worry that my daughter may die. Yet at the same time, log-cabin is easy to sew and quite rhythmic in its nature.

Although this activity is not going to take away the problems or even fix them, by doing something which was purposeful and distracted me, it gave me some calm and peaceful space in my life.

The need to feel useful

If you have lived with a health condition that can't be fixed, pain that you cannot take away or cared for another person who has, you will understand the importance of the next purpose.

I started feeling useless – Erica was in pain for about two years and as her mother, I had to watch that, unable to do much. I felt useless. With sewing, I have found that it gives me a sense of achievement and as a result, my feelings about my own self-worth are given a real boost. When Erica still lived at home, we had carers come in 24 hours a day – I often shared with them what I had made which, of course, gave me a positive feeling. I made gifts for a number of her carers – so appreciated – that once again I could lose that feeling of being a useless person.

Building my own social network

Finally, I have met some wonderful people and made some new friends through my interest. I love going to dressmaking classes, quilting workshops or retreats where I am just 'me' – I am not Erica's mum or a disability expert – I am just one member in the group. I can share some of my life as a carer if I want to, or I can just be me.

The therapeutic activity that is UK Quilters United

I take an active role on both the UK Quilters United Facebook group, as an admin for the Continuing Development sub-group and I blog for the website. Through this I have become friendly, both in reality and virtually, with a completely new group of people. Being involved has also utilised some of the skills I used when I worked – so once again, it feeds into my self-worth.

I have been careful to talk about my sewing as a 'therapeutic activity' rather than a 'therapy'. Therapy, if effective, will 'fix' a mental health issue and 'therapeutic activity' will alleviate the stress, and it is the latter that I am referring to.

I know there are a lot of quilters who live with a disability or long-term health condition, or are carers or have other major life challenges – so I hope this chapter has resonance for you.

Find me online at ukqu.co.uk/members/jeannecarlin/blog

Houses on the Hill

Quilts for care leavers

By Maggie Lloyd-Jones

In the dim and distant past, I used to sew everything by hand and I mean everything; sheets, curtains, clothes, pretty binding on shoes. At one point, I started a patchwork top – hexagons - didn't we all? Forty odd years after I last sewed anything, I was about to be a retired child solicitor, and I'd promised myself and told everyone when they asked how I was going to spend my retirement, that I would spoil my grandson and start to quilt. So, I began to build up my stash. I still had the not inconsiderable stash in my cupboard from years ago, but tastes change, and I became a fabric addict.

I began to make quilts, lap quilts, table runners and place mats, all for charity or to raise funds for whatever, as well as making quilts for my grandson. He loved and still loves, the quilts I make for him. My best customer so far, along with his brother, but my daughter does not want me to make more, and neither does my brother. Sound familiar?

Then the Lemn Sissay Foundation (since May 2019 called *The Gold from the Stone Foundation*) came to my attention. Amongst other things, it encourages cities to support its care leavers by holding Christmas Day dinners for those who would otherwise be alone on that day - all volunteer led and self-funded. My friend Liz Fossu was chair of the Leeds steering committee, and I supported Leeds for a couple of years as I had worked there. In 2018, I made a quilt for auction at their first fundraising Dinner for the Christmas Day Dinner, rather than spending the money on the cost of going to the dinner. That fund raiser was in September 2018.

The Eureka moment

Roll backwards to 26th August 2018, and I was at the recording of the part of the Channel 4 programme called Superkids, the part which covered Lemn talking about his life in the care system in Wigan: his mother had come to the UK from Ethiopia to study, gave birth to Lemn, and asked for help whilst she finished her studies. And then Lemn became "lost" in the system, despite her wanting her son home.

What struck a chord and caused me to have my Eureka moment, was hearing Lemn say that when at the age of twelve he was placed in residential care from long term foster care, all he'd wanted was a hug.

- A hug -

In the dark in that small theatre, my immediate thought was – 'I make hugs, I can do something about this.' I spoke to Liz and her steering committee were very enthusiastic. I spoke to Amy Watson who had been involved with the Grenfell Towers appeal and ran the GT Quilters Facebook page, to see what she thought of the idea, and she agreed to support and help. The idea? To provide a quilt to each of the care leavers who attended the 2018 Christmas Day dinners to be held in Leeds and if at all possible to cover Manchester as well, as this is where my own grown children live. Fifty guests at each dinner - 100 quilts in less than 12 weeks. No pressure then….

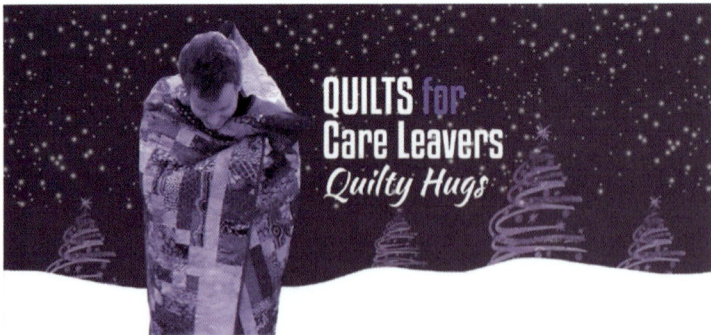

The response to the call

The initial Quilts for Christmas Dinners Facebook page was set up on 6th October 2018. I invited my Facebook quilting friends to join, posted the information on all the UK quilting sites I was a member of and asked others to do the same. I sat back to wait. I didn't have to wait long, to be honest; some could not help that year but would the next. Some helped or offered financial or fabric donations. I asked for longarmers – just in case – and four people with frames came up trumps, along with two who were prepared to wrangle quilts through their domestic machines. I took in quilts of all sizes, along with orphan blocks and otherwise unwanted tops. Some quilts were too large to meet my goal of providing a hug, and so they are on one side until they are (possibly) to be auctioned to raise funds.

A preferred size was set: minimum 44" wide up to max 54", and at least 66" long, preferably 72" or even longer – to provide a hug rather than overwhelm.

At the UKQU web site bloggers retreat, I asked for an hour of their time to help me match and sew donated blocks together. Many worked on the project all Saturday and Sunday, some taking blocks away to make into quilts.

All or nothing

We played an amazing game of UK quilt tag. By mid-December, I had sufficient quilts to gift to Leeds, and nearly enough for Manchester. I was quite sad to see my babies be collected. I will only agree to provide quilts to dinners if there are enough for every guest attending to have the choice of taking one or not. By December 22nd, Manchester was covered and I had a few spares. Barnsley was holding its first dinner and 17 quilts would be ideal. I was also able to supply a special one to Wigan.

These things I could do. I became Mrs Claus on Christmas Eve, with my hubby a willing elf. Christmas Day was traumatic, waiting to hear about the reactions of the younglings.

Not all those referred by social care arrive at the dinners, and I accept that it is a very traumatic time for many. Some people are referred for a second and even a third time. But would anyone choose to take a quilt? At the event, they were laid out, unwrapped, for the guests to choose their own. What they were and why they were gifted was explained.

Only one (!!!) person out of all those who attended the three dinners decided not to take a quilt. I was sent pictures and indeed videos of those choosing their quilts and telling me why they had done so. I shared those pictures and videos on the Facebook group page of care leavers thanking us.

Working as a team

This is a team effort, make no mistake. Whilst the aim of The Foundation is for local communities to support 'their own' care leavers between the ages of 18 and 25, we do not (yet) have sufficient members to support all the local dinners, and not every town or county holds such a dinner (yet). Whist the intention is to keep quilts as local as possible to where they have been made, we cannot currently always achieve this. So, quilts move around the country, hopefully not as far as during the first year in 2018. Another problem for us logistically is that dinner committees often do not set up before September each year. I have a good idea where dinners will be held from the previous year, but new ones are always coming on board, and I'm delighted to say that some of those are as a direct result of this group.

What about our team? Some folk quilt from the completed top through to finished quilts. Others will piece tops and then the tops plus backing go off to our longarmers who are provided with wadding by the project. This is provided from our fund raising and super support from EQS and Empress, specifically. Longarmers tend to supply their own threads and quilt away. We have some binding fairies, too. Sewing Days are being set up all over the country, as well as virtual group days. Much cake is provided and enjoyed!!

Our members come from anywhere in the UK. Some like me, used to work in the legal sector involved in child protection, others might be social workers, foster carers, care leavers, or those working with care leavers, City and Guild tutors or students, professional longarmers or fabric sellers, as well as people who have had no contact with the social care system at all. Many are retired, many had lost their sewing mojo for a while - but have found a focus for their time and that stash of fabrics saved over years. This is especially so when there is no one to make for.

The makers online community

We have two Facebook groups: one is a public group *Quilts for Christmas Dinners*, and there is a closed group at *Quilts for Care leavers makers*. The names are different because in due course, I hope that we can grow large enough to provide quilts for care leavers as they leave care, whether they are referred to the Christmas Day dinners under the auspices of The Foundation or not. We are not yet a charity, but are working on it.

In the makers' Facebook group, we share fabric, orphan blocks looking for their forever home, patterns, and problems. One of the reasons for this group being a closed group, is that members need to feel comfortable enough to tell us things that they may not feel able to do so elsewhere. Many have said that they feel a personal connection to the project. The group is there to be supportive and help us share and often, have a laugh and occasionally a rant. Both sites are there to help raise awareness of the situation of care leavers, and provide some education as to what we can do to help.

I've been told some amazing stories, most of them uplifting, but all a privilege to have heard.

What has not ceased to amaze me is the open hearts and willingness of our quilting community to help others in need. Of course, there are others out there in our local or national community who would benefit from a quilty hug. These younglings are not in need because of their own actions.

The quilts we make, remind them that they are loved, even by people who they are unlikely to ever meet. What is an additional pay off was the most unexpected and unlooked for one: the renaissance of the love of quilting by people who had lost that spark and reason to quilt, as well as the forging of new friendships. Thank you, Facebook.

We have a common purpose, and long may it last!!

Find out more online at www.facebook.com/QuiltsforChristmasDinners

MADE JUST FOR YOU
To keep you warm and cosy
Remember, you are loved
From Quilts for Christmas Dinners
2018

Life experiences

A keepsake quilter

By Katie Done

I have always had an interest in crafts and I got more into sewing in my late teens. After making myself a lot of clothes, I found I had a growing pile of scraps which I wanted to make use of, so I made my first quilt. As a result, I developed a love of quilting. To feed my habit and have a reason to sew things, I set up a Facebook page and started to attend regular craft fairs.

When life got busier and I became pregnant, I decided I needed to think more long-term, with the aim on staying at home with my little man. I loved my day-job with the Alzheimer's Society, but I was travelling a lot around Lincolnshire and it wasn't practical with a little one at home. After having George, I developed a greater appreciation for the fabrics and patterns in children's clothes and what a great quilt they would make.

Making my first keepsake quilt

Four months into motherhood and I decided I'd like to create a quilt from baby clothes. I made a couple of small practice quilts with baby vests I wasn't as keen on and had been well worn and not much good to anyone else. George hadn't grown out of many of my favourite outfits by this time, so I asked a good friend of mine if she had any old clothes from her little ones she wouldn't mind me turning into a quilt. Much to my surprise, she was more than happy to donate all her favourite clothes to me. This was the start of what has today become a small business which I fit in around family life.

My keepsake quilt business was born

Looking back, I must have been crazy taking on such a task with a four-month old baby. However, as he didn't move much back then, it was reasonably easy to work around him. Actually, I was more motivated

91

to make it work because of him; spending time with this little dude rather than going back to work really pushed me to grow my business.

Two years later, I am really proud of how far it has come and I am currently working on my 100th keepsake.

It hasn't been easy and now when my little man is nearly three years old, I am very much looking forward to seeing what I can achieve whilst he is at nursery more hours.

My quilting has definitely improved a lot since I started even though I had made plenty of quilts before the first keepsake. My head is full of new ideas and quilt designs, to help me stand out from the crowd of keepsake creators, so I am not likely by be bored any time soon!

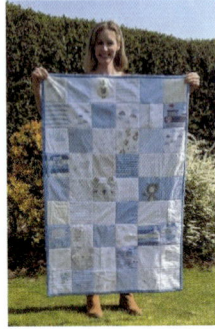

Tips for making your own keepsake quilt

Sewing a keepsake quilt with your kid's clothes is often what inspires people to get into sewing and quilting in the first place. This is a great starting point!

If I was to give any tips, it would be to make a few other projects before you start cutting into your most precious clothes. Whether that is using normal quilting cotton or baby clothes that aren't as special, it doesn't really matter.

When it comes to creating your actual keepsake, the most important thing is to stabilise them with iron on interfacing first. Clothes stretch differently, so it is crucial that you use stabiliser to keep your sewing accurate.

Find me online at www.thefabricsquirrel.com

Artisan textile and screen printing designer

By Colette Moscrop

I am a textile designer and screen printer, creating original fabrics for modern makers. I print with rich colours onto natural fabrics – the cotton and linen base cloths are perfect for quilting, embroidery and many craft projects.

I am inspired by urban architecture, the colours of nature and styles from the 1920s through 1950s. A Scandinavian influence shows through my work with simple shapes being a recurring element. I love florals and I like to incorporate these into my designs more. I recently introduced a stylised tulip print, which has been well received, particularly with embroiderers keen to add their favourite colours with thread to make the fabric more personal.

Rich, juicy colours excite me and I love to pair solid-coloured fabrics with my prints to really make the designs stand out. I mix my ink colours by hand to get just the perfect shade. They are all water based and eco-friendly (and washable).

Using Mum's fabric scraps

Like many of us, my story began as a child making clothes for my dolls with my Mum's fabric scraps. Textiles continued to be a part of my creative life and after studying Fashion Design at art college, I worked in the industry until I had my two daughters. As a stay-at-home mum, I started to appreciate the everyday textiles that surround us and began to embellish and make practical items out of my favourite fabrics – dresses for my girls, a Liberty peg bag, embroidered tea towels – and a host of new cushions popped up around the house. A simple, cheerful object could suddenly bring joy to the most mundane chores.

The Modern Quilt Guild and vintage cushions

Around this time, I joined the London Modern Quilt Guild as a way to meet other people with a passion for textiles and sewing. I combined vintage fabrics with my children's outgrown clothing and began to make my first quilted cushions. I took a Guild workshop on screen printing and fell in love with the process of putting my own designs on fabric. I experimented, had failures, learnt from my mistakes and continued to grow as a textile artist.

Polygon play cushion using my own fabrics

Setting up my own business

I had previously run my own corsetry and evening wear business and began to use my experience and background in fashion to develop my hobby into a business.

I took the leap and started selling the fabrics I was printing on Etsy and when photos started to appear of the items people were making with them, I was overjoyed. Knowing that people choose my fabrics carefully for their projects is an incredible feeling and I am proud to play a small part in the process of another maker's journey.

I have a garden studio, which allows me to work easily around family life. It's a little creative hub where my mind can focus on the next project free from distractions. In there, I work on new designs by hand, using pencil, paper and ink. It's also where I do all of the hand screen printing, sewing and where I run workshops. My large workbench transforms weekly from desk to print table depending on my schedule. I'm very fortunate to have such a flexible space.

Screen printed and ready for a customer

Future artisan plans

Keeping a craft alive and creating artisan fabrics is a time-consuming and labour-intensive process and I hope to grow and to develop the business further over the coming years. I'm planning some new kits and would like to share ideas with other makers and inspire them to use my fabrics in a way that's unique to each individual. Creating personal and meaningful items is a way to connect with my craft and expand my skill set while producing something truly beautiful.

I am a big fan of hand stitching. Connecting with the fabric and adding another dimension of texture is really important to me. I have created a small series of mini pieces in which I use up small off-cuts and misprints to create a textile collage. I back them with cotton batting and hand embroider over them to create some interesting quilted textures. These may become wall hangings, or placemats, I'm not sure yet, but I am thoroughly enjoying the process.

Making useful, thoughtful items

On a personal level, making more thoughtful projects is currently on my mind, investing my time and energy into making something that will add value to our lives in the home. I am planning a table runner at the moment – I will piece together lots of my apple green prints and hand quilt and embroider onto this over the coming months. It will be a slow project, but when it's complete it will be an original piece we can all enjoy around the dinner table.

Find me online at colettemoscrop.com

Chance of a Lifetime

By Sue Creasy

Travel to learn. Return to inspire.

This was my experience.

In 2012 my husband and I were at a dinner party with friends, when one of those seated was enthusing about his recent trip to Hong Kong and Australia looking at bus electronic timetables and travel. He had been awarded a scholarship by the Winston Churchill Memorial Trust, and he started to encourage me to apply for a scholarship myself - as in his words, 'I was the kind of ambassador they were looking for'.

Applying for a scholarship

The scholarship is available to any British citizen, regardless of age and 100 of these are awarded annually in ten different categories.

My husband and children, then aged 18 and 16, were fully supportive and encouraged me to apply. There were a lot of stages to go through, but I was called for an interview at Hyde Park Corner in London. On arrival I was told that over 1,900 applicants had applied over the ten different categories, but a staggering 670 had applied in the same category as I had. Out of these, 100 had been called for interview for ten available scholarships. I had applied in the Creative Arts category to study Colour, Construction, Design and Embellishment of Church Banners, in the United States.

Quilting skills helped me during interview

A quilt is made of three layers and a number of the banners I had previously made would hang as wall quilts - so in answering questions at the interview, I commented that I could hang a church banner one day for a funeral and the next day for a wedding, changing the setting and atmosphere; they were pleased with that answer.

They had expected stage managers and choreographers to apply in this category, not a quilt and banner maker!!

At this point I need you to realise that I had never travelled away without my family, had never travelled for more than a week and had never been to America!

Planning the trip

Eight weeks later, in February, I heard that I had been successful and could start planning my trip. Timing for me was the most important factor; my daughter was off to university in late September, so I planned to travel once she was settled.

The main event in the planning was to visit the International Quilt Show in Houston, held every October or November. I wanted to be able to attend classes, but to be honest, to attend the largest quilt show in the world, was a dream come true.

The scholarship included a substantial grant to travel for up to eight weeks, which I managed to budget for, including all accommodation, visits, flights and essential purchases..!

I assisted a producer with stage management of a Christmas production of The Messiah, I attended lectures, visited museums, took a three-day class on shibori and fabric construction and explored different approaches to fabric, paint and design.

I flew over 14,000 miles, visited six different States (Texas, Oklahoma, Kentucky, Tennessee, Florida, and Virginia Beach), took eleven different flights, drove 1,500 miles in three different cars, and slept in twelve different beds.

Inspiring others

On my return, my commitment was to inspire my community and write a report about my experiences. Personally, I gained in confidence and increased my belief in my own abilities.

The scholarship also opened up opportunities for me to develop a teaching course called, Permission to play - exploring various creative techniques' Out of this course grew a church based patchwork and quilting group called PieceMakers, who continue to meet on the fourth Friday of every month.

I am grateful to my dinner acquaintance who encouraged me to apply and to the Winston Churchill Memorial Trust, for selecting me.; it truly was an amazing experience.

Quilting passion and inheritance

By Sue Allaway

My late mum, once she retired, began making quilts. She must have made over 20 for various close friends and relations. I wonder now, what has happened to all of them? Are they still loved and appreciated, used on beds and cuddled into, or do they lay forgotten in an airing cupboard? Have they been gifted to others or found their way to an appreciative home via a charity shop?

Mum never kept a record, neither photographic or written, about who she had made quilts for, so if anyone reading this has a quilt with hand embroidered 'Marian Harding' and the year it was made, you'll know it will have been made by my mum! I am originally from Falmouth in Cornwall, but now live in Torquay in Devon, so many of the quilts may still be in this area of the country.

Mum passed on her passion for quilting

I've inherited my mum's passion for quilting, but sadly not her beautifully neat hand embroidery stitches, or her eye for colour in quilts. She passed on the confidence to be creative and a bit non-conformist!

I still have one quilt she made in 1992. It was made for a single bed so it's rather dwarfed on a king sized double as in the photo!

When I was sorting through the family home, I found a charm pack and some unfinished, but pieced hexagonal blocks. I've used these to create a loose cover for my combined desk and sewing chair, meaning that mum is always close by when I am sitting at my desk.

Sorting out her sewing box was hard, it all felt so very personal! I've passed the sewing box onto my sister in law, Lorna, along with mum's sewing machine, at mum's request, since she was very fond of Lorna, and a fan of her very creative costumes for carnivals and other fancy dress events.

100

Before passing on the sewing box, I did take out and keep one item that I now use. I found the needle case, that I made, probably in the late 1960's from fabric left over from an A-line dress I would have made for myself, with my mum's help. The fabric is still in its prime. It is rather bright, as the photo of the inside of the case shows. The purple is crimplene, but I've got no recollection of what it had been made into originally; possibly an evening dress, since my parents were very active members of the Round Table.

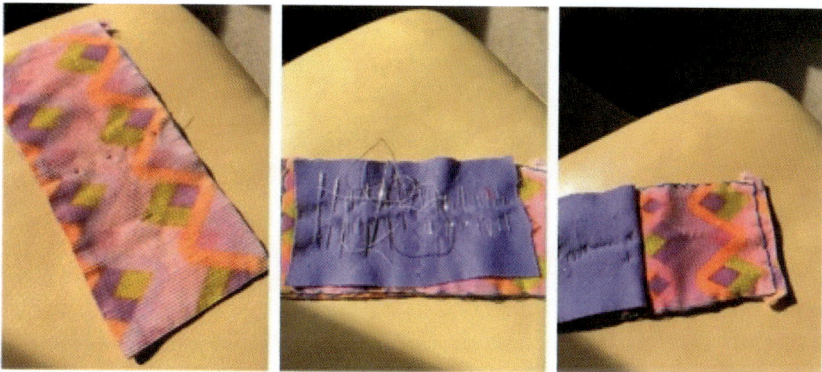

The needle case I made over 50 years ago

This quilt is inspired by Dartmoor and the fabrics I had at home.

I used techniques inspired by Jane Hopkins, whose courses I always felt very privileged to go on! It started as a door cover, then a Roman blind and now it hangs on the wall in our stairwell (the only wall tall enough to fit it).

'That Old Bag' – from a shoulder's perspective

By Teresa Barrow

My name is Scapula Genoid, which might seem a bit strange to you, but basically, I am the bit between the arm and the neck that makes the arm work. Other definitions are interesting, for example you can give someone the cold shoulder, you can be a shoulder to cry on, or you can even shoulder someone out of the way. During my existence as her shoulder, I have seen a few things I tell you, some happy, and some very sad, during the considerable time I have been around. I am the left shoulder by the way, there is a right one as well, but they don't do an awful lot these days, something to do with being too sloping, lower than me, and attached to other bits that don't work too well. Now I am not being 'shoulderist' in any way, as I am sure they mean well and try very hard for her, but they just can't cut the mustard when faced with shouldering responsibility and duties the way, I, her left shoulder can.

Plenty of knickers, but no beach bag...

It is a bit mean just calling the thing I am attached to just 'her', so I will give her a name, it is TOB, short for 'That Old Bat'. She has been called a lot worse, believe me, so I am being extremely kind here.

Let me introduce you to 'That Old Bag'; it all started on holiday in a posh hotel's gift shop. TOB had packed everything including enough clean knickers to appear dignified, should she be run over by a whole fleet of buses, as her mother had taught her. What was lacking in her 22.9 Kilo bag (23 kilo is the max allowance, so she made it by a whisker), was the all-important beach bag. Her adoring husband of course offered to buy one for her in the hotel boutique, but being a sensible lass, she said no, once she saw the price tags. Instead she carried on using the plastic duty free carrier bag with a towel wrapped around it for modesty issues and to avoid embarrassment.

So, a plan was hatched. If she could make quilts, she could make a bag of course, but it had to be somewhat different from any bag ever made before by any quilter. It had to be mahoosively huge, so it could also double as a picnic rug sort of sit-upon-thingy for attending open air music events, because she can't stand for more than a few minutes. It also had to have wide squidgy soft straps, because she was being kind to me, her dear left shoulder. I get all the hard work of course, because the right one can't even manage a teensy handbag without the bag falling off.

Dithering and hoarding, TOB style

But TOB as ever had to make it ultra-difficult, it had to match her favourite top too. She auditioned lots of hopeful wannabe fabrics by purchasing them, stroking them (what's all that about... really?), until a decision was made on a certain range of batik fabrics. She bought not just enough to make a bag, but probably at least enough to make another 50, just in case 'That Old Bag' #1 ever wore out, got lost, got bagnapped, or a football or rugby stadium needed a new colourful pre-match cover for the grass.

Well 'That Old Bag' was duly finished and it then returned to a remote island in the Caribbean just in time for a fabulous blues music festival on the beach. It went shopping too and was sturdy enough to carry 24 Carib beers, and numerous other essentials from the super-market. As TOB's shoulder, I have to say that even with the soft wide squidgy straps, she was pushing her luck on that one, it really hurt! It then even out-blinged a local celebrity known for his rather creative dress sense, but was much admired by lots of people.

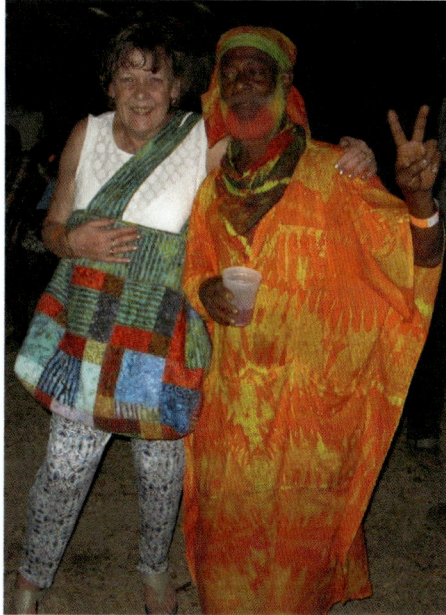

A bit of a celebrity captured by the paparazzi

'That Old Bag' has had its own photo shoots, it has been to TOB's local supermarket for shopping on a regular basis, it has gone abroad a lot as hand baggage, with other stuff shoved inside it. It has been in and out of the washing machine goodness knows how many times and still it keeps on going! It has also been asked to host a new blog series on the ukqu.co.uk website. No killing 'That Old Bag' despite constant abuse and extreme usage conditions.

Not content with making a bag to match her top, TOB found a matching car in St Tropez and suggested that this unique concept BMW model would make a perfect present; a request sadly denied. A great lunch followed by way of consolation for the non-purchase of the car. I can confirm that just to my left was one of the best-known film stars in the world, the amazing Brigitte Bardot. That was a bit awesome and I was a lot closer to her than TOB's right shoulder, but I digress.

Back home she finally used some of the matching stash to make a real picnic blanket which has been used many times on the grass, over knees and around me, her shoulder, and other special friends' shoulders too. Us shoulders are very generous and like to share the hugs.

Some jobs are harder than others, even for a bag

'That Old Bag' has had some tough journeys to make on my shoulder too; the absolute worst one was taking her Darling Daddy's best going out clothes to the nursing home where he later died. This was just so she could dress him, so he could be all shipshape and tickety boo, for his final ever journey. This journey was not without surprises however, there was an Oxfordshire Art Week exhibition going on there in the main lounge. A lady that TOB had spoken to in the preceding days while admiring her amazing textile art, called out as she passed, 'I love your bag'. TOB turned around with waterfalls running down her face and that lady knew instantly what had just happened. I got huge hugs and I got extremely wet with her tears too. Shoulders to cry on are always handy in such situations.

Faithful, but not always getting it right

On a brighter note, TOB is nothing but faithful to 'That Old Bag' and just yesterday she took it shopping with a friend in the remote island place where the idea originated. Her friend commented, 'So you still have 'That Old Bag'?'.

I have to report however that TOB's ability to get even a simple shopping task completed successfully are still an absolute zero as normal. Well, guess who bought baby milk formula for infants needing extra vitamins after weaning and not using Mummy's milk anymore, instead of normal powdered dried milk for coffee? Yes TOB, but of course it was only to be expected given her track record. She has more 'form' in doing all the wrong things for all the right reasons, than most thoroughbred race-horses could ever achieve form-wise.

So nice she had to do it twice! The Shame!

TOB pulled an absolute blinder today, if I had known what she was about to do I would have made 'That Old Bag' hide under the bed or in the wardrobe! The absolute cheek of it! She rocks up at the Golden Rock Inn in that remote island place for lunch. Greeted on arrival as a valued new client, she then had the temerity to ask for her normal table! The Maître D' inquired as to which table that was. TOB replied …

'Oh just the stone gazebo on the patio, you know the one, the one we had lunch under on December 6th 2015, the day after we got married.'

TOB's husband is by now seriously contemplating joining the nifty beautiful heron by diving into the pool to catch fish, just to avoid embarrassment. Now, in restaurant terms that iconic gazebo is somewhat akin to flying economy and expecting to be automatically upgraded to First Class with fluffy slippers, sleepsuit, a comfy bed and of course champagne on ice! It IS the symbol of the Golden Rock Inn. Of course, TOB got her table and after they cleared the other four place settings, they both had a very agreeable lunch.

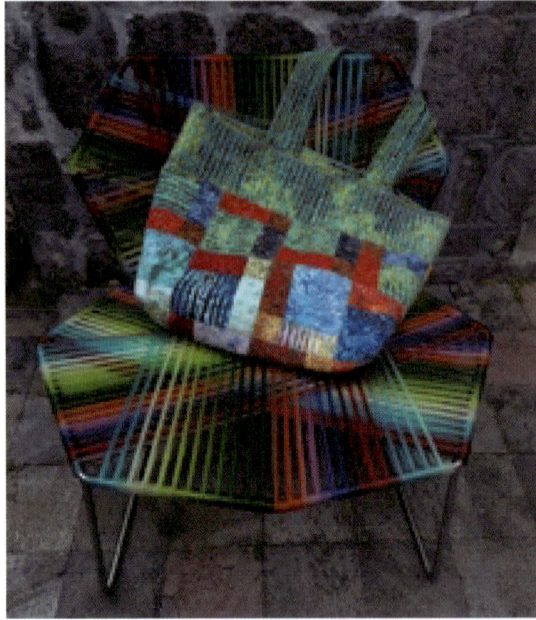

Then it all just went downhill. TOB spotted a chair, not just any old chair, but a very expensive chair, part of the art collection of New York artists Helen & Price Marden who own the Golden Rock.

"Oh, look it matches 'That Old Bag'!", she said.

I am ashamed to say as her shoulder, I actually let her take 'That Old Bag' there, to do a sneaky photo shoot because I actually thought it was a great match in terms of colour. Now if only she would stop winging on about how she thought of the colour combo first, and chickens and eggs and stuff, I would be a happy shoulder.

You will need a boat for at least part of the way, but it is TOB's little slice of secret heaven and that is how it is staying! There are only occasional disputes over sunbeds and that is fine because the other occupants are equally chilled!

Many more adventures to come

Despite being constantly attached to this woman, my personal 'That Old Bat', I'm actually quite fond of her, quirks and all. She makes me shake with giggles and laughter as she blunders on from one total disaster to another. I would not be anyone else's left shoulder because she is loving, kind and generous, and I hope I am around long enough to witness more interesting adventures on our mutual journey together. I have no doubt we will of course be accompanied by 'That Old Bag' as well.

Find me online at ukqu.co.uk/members/nostalgianeedlework/blog

How a painter became a quilter

By Judith Clarke

I always enjoyed playing with pencils and colouring as a child. Although materials were not plenty when I was growing up, I remember getting a bumper colouring book and crayons in my stocking every Christmas. I also have a very strong memory of my dad buying my three brothers and me a present each from himself, no idea why. I opened mine to find a printing set. I was over the moon. Then one of my brothers opened his to find he had a knitting set. I was mortified that we had to swap! I remember doing collage at school and the pleasure it gave, although I was never really encouraged to make more than was needed in class.

At secondary school my best friend and I decided to make comics for each other, including a free gift that was included on the cover. My comic was based around art and drawing. I took O-level art, but didn't surpass, and wasn't encouraged to take it any further.

Life took over and I didn't draw again until after my first child was born. Determined back in the early 80s to keep my identity and not become just someone's mother and wife, I joined our local arts workshop that had a crèche. My love of creating was nurtured here, as well as it being my 'me time'. Over the years I tried all mediums and eventually settled on oils, mainly because me and glass and three small children didn't mix. And the smell.... mmmmm, such a wonderful smell, oil paints, linseed oil.......

Experimenting and searching

I was always experimenting, searching, but I didn't know for what. But each painting led to another, a different style, subject, who knows what I was looking for. I started painting with a pallet knife, thick and luscious paint. Yummy. I did many courses, my curiosity insatiable. There were times I longed for a time machine to go back and talk with Leonardo, Van Gogh, Monet, Bonnard and many more.

110

Family holidays started to become in search of where they lived and painted, where they rested. Apart from my family it was all I thought about.

I found my own subjects during and after taking a degree in fine art, of which I had to take a couple of textile modules. The subjects that fascinated me most were the landscape, and the folklore and stories attached to it.

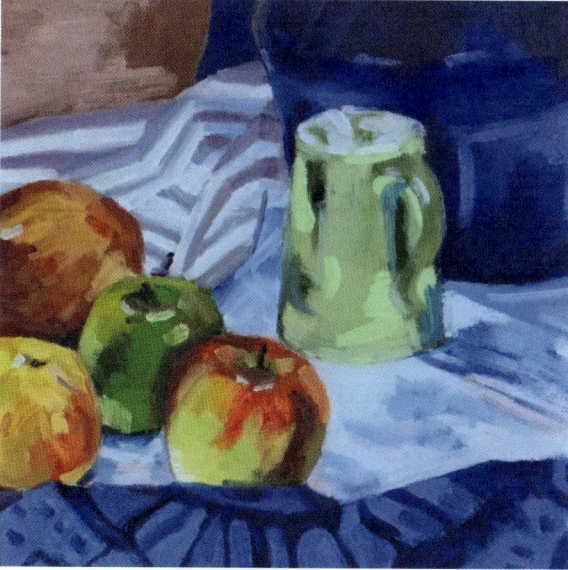

Relocating and reassessing my life

My family originated from Derbyshire and North Yorkshire, although brought up in the Midlands I started to long to return home, as by now the Derbyshire family lived in North Yorkshire.

The loss of my mum in 2003 prompted a re-think and we moved to Whitby in 2007. It was hard, as family were now no longer with us, just a couple of cousins left in this corner of God's Own Country. But it was now home and we have never felt it to be anything else. I soon found although there are many artists here, they work quite singularly. We do have an active Art Society which is great.

We now run a B&B, so that took priority and most of our time my creativity took a large back seat. I also found that the wonderful smells I adored were not conducive to people coming on holiday!

111

Discovering art quilting

Four years on and I lost my dad who had moved with us. This meant I had a room, sadly but finally, to call my own. I reached out to find that local creative groups, other than the Art Society, were mainly quilters. I joined a local group, although I had never worked in this way. I was looked on as a little strange. I attended a couple of local classes on how to make quilts but almost immediately started to put my own spin on them. People soon realised that I wasn't to be pigeonholed and I had discovered art quilting. My paintings became quilts, where my paint is now fabric and thread.

I approach my quilts in the same way a painter would a painting, and I have found my 'go to' is whole cloth, with appliqué, which I see as my ground (or background) and drawing!

I also seem to default to black thread a lot of the time, which I have linked back to those childhood colouring books.

Gulliver and Gail, by me, the Seagull Woman

Whitby, where I live, is a magical place. Full of folklore, sunny and windswept days, spray from the sea, fish and chips and the sound of the gulls. Unable at first to express my creativity in the ways which I was used to, I sketched and thought and plotted. Out of my thoughts came stories. The first stories were full of magic and mermaids, witches and Dracula. They were made at first, for my nieces and nephews, in order that they would come to know our and their grandfather's new home. The younger of them were not old enough to appreciate the stories, so I made up tales about seagulls, one of which was called Gulliver.

Gulliver has stuck and he has since married his first love, Gail. They both feature in my quilts and I have become known as the seagull woman!

Many a time, I am approached and asked if it is me who makes the seagulls. Yes, Gulliver now colours my days. He is with me in thoughts as well as in my work. His stories are becoming my stories and we tell them together.

Still a painter, but now using fabric and thread

So, there you have it, I'm still a painter, but as I now use fabric and thread as my medium, I must be a quilt painter! Yes, I have also painted on quilts…

I'm experimenting with dying my own fabric and am an avid up-cycler. Who knows what the future will hold, but I know it's definitely full of experimental quilty fun.

Find me online at ukqu.co.uk/members/judithsemporium/blog

Notes from an expat in Spain

By Sue Burford

Who'd have thought it? I must admit when I saw the post on Facebook asking for volunteer writers for the book, I immediately thought it was something I would love to do. Then, I got the jitters and thought 'No, it is not for me'.

However, here I am writing this story for the second book by and about UK Quilters United, so I thought I would introduce myself properly… my name is Susan Burford – known to all as Sue. I am a year past my 70th birthday and have never been so busy. I have been doing patchwork and quilting for only a few years, but I have always made my own clothes and those of the children when they were small and when labels weren't so important ☺.

Relocating to Spain

My other half and I took early retirement 19 years ago and moved to sunny Spain to live the DREAM! We live here in Granada Province, in Andalucía, in a cave house. I have never regretted our decision to leave the United Kingdom. However, I do miss the friendliness and camaraderie of like-minded people who enjoy sewing and crafty makes.

Quilting and patchwork here in Spain is almost non-existent and locating fabrics, especially 100% cottons, is difficult, but I have been able to convince a small family-owned shop in the next town to stock some Robert Kaufman designs…. If I can get them to stock jelly rolls, charm packs and suchlike, I will be in my element. As an alternative, I buy online from some of the wonderful suppliers back in the United Kingdom.

114

A typical cave house in Castillejar, Spain

Finding online like-minded friends

When I joined the various UKQU Facebook groups, never did I think that I would be rewarded with the great friends I have made over the past three years. Although, we have never met, we have so much in common and 'speak' almost daily!

Learning patchwork and quilting with the help of these new friends has been a joy. Whatever query I have, answers flow in, giving me new ideas and new ways of doing things.

I spend many hours designing, sewing and finishing various projects in my very own workroom out in the garden. Inspiration for my favourite landscape wall hangings, is all around me and I explore this in my blog on the UKQU website on a regular basis.

Keeping busy

Before starting quilting and patchwork, the only blocks I knew about were the ones you use to build walls with; jelly rolls and fat quarters were things you covered up well with blouses (!!!) and a charm pack was a selection of little silver figures on a bracelet. Little did I know they would take over my life.

The past twelve months have been very busy; I have made seven quilts and various postcards and hexies. I was also privileged to make and receive my very first mini swap quilt!

Thank you to everyone I have 'met' - I truly appreciate you all.

Find me online at ukqu.co.uk/members/fabricologist/blog

This is a mini quilt I originally made for one of the UKQU swaps;
but as I liked it too much, I made something else for my swap partner

Paella, my birthday lunch on my special birthday

Quilting alone around the world

By Linda Lane Thornton

For eleven years, while undertaking a circumnavigation on our yacht, the SV Coromandel, I produced a journal quilt every month of the journey. I was quite happy working in isolation from the quilting community; I seldom met other sailing quilters – only two in eleven years – but I sought out textiles everywhere we went.

I spent a lovely day in Moorea, the island next to Tahiti, with a lady who made *tifaifai* (appliquéd leaves, fruit and flowers) also known as *tivaevae* in the Cook Islands where the art is more widely known. I joined a quilting group during our six-month sojourn in New Zealand and I visited the Calico Christmas Quiltfest in Auckland with them.

Seeking the safety of the quilt displays

Spending six months in the Chesapeake Bay area of the eastern United States gave me the opportunity of going to the American Quilters' Society show in Chattanooga, Tennessee, where I was so bewildered by the fabrics, notions, patterns and machines that I fled to the quilt display areas, spending only $5 during the course of the day and that on a tee-shirt!

Analysing my feelings during a much-needed coffee-break, I realised that I had been out of touch with the quilting world for a LONG time! Yes, I'd had access to quilting magazines, usually in one swoop, as they were all delivered to my brother's house north of Cape Town in South Africa, so I got them all at once and usually had to read them while I was there to avoid excess baggage charges (see page 33). I didn't bother looking at the new equipment sections – after all, to where would I have them sent and how would I be able to store them on the good ship Coromandel?

The net result of this is that I realised, that during my travels things had moved forward a great deal. I don't know what half of the notions are: Westalee rulers? A Sizzix? Do I need any of these? Will I be unfrocked if I don't have one? Am I disenfranchised?

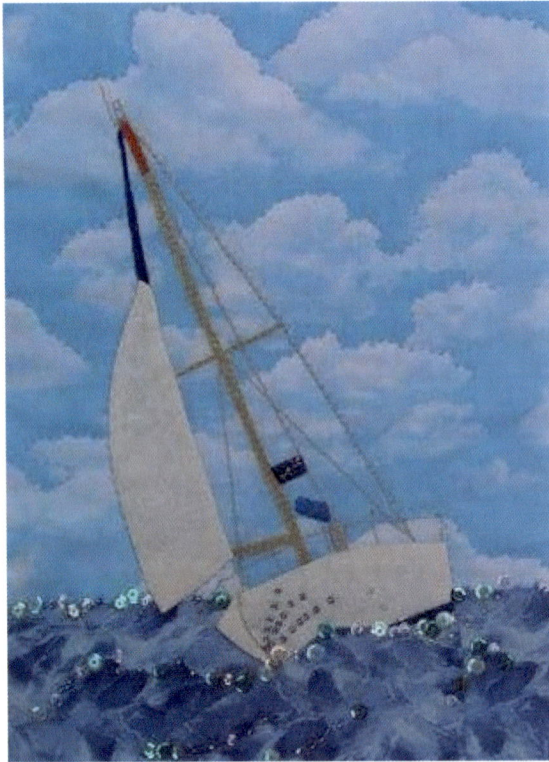

One of my journal quilts

The failed hard sell

I recall a very nice man at the Chattanooga Quilt Show trying to sell me a long-arm quilting machine; to me, who lived on a 35-foot sailing boat. "I'm sure you could fit it on board," he said.

Well, yes, of course I could get it on board. But then the question would arise about where Andy and I would LIVE because the machine would take up the whole of the saloon. Eventually I asked, "Will it work on a 12-volt battery system?"

That finally shut him up.

Realising I don't need fancy gadgets

Later on, I spent a couple of months back in England when we had decided to sell our house there and move abroad permanently. I joined a group of quilters in Blyth, the Hotch Patch Quilters, who not only welcomed me as warmly as a rackful of toast, but often had me in stitches with their chat. I watched these ladies and the incredible things they were making and realised that I didn't need the latest gadgets or the newest notions. In the few weeks I was there, I stitched a quilt top, by hand as usual, and enjoyed every minute of it.

Yes, I have a machine, but sewing machines have always scared the willies out of me. I cannot stitch a straight line even when the line is marked on the fabric. My free-motion quilting is uneven, jagged, untidy and uninspiring, and just not FUN.

In my happy place

So, I'm happy in my little world. Access to the internet means that I can look at all sorts of goodies, visit any number of virtual quilt shows, be inspired by the work of others, yet I seldom spend more than about half an hour a day on the computer. I'd rather be making something by hand that I know I can achieve, than looking at quilts and wall hangings that need a truckload of gadgets to bring to fruition. It's all too easy to feel left behind in the gadget stakes, as if the quality of one's work depends on having access to the latest technology.

Whenever I feel like this I recall a block patchwork quilt I saw in the Virginia Quilt Museum in Harrisonburg. It was made in the Civil War era (1861–65) and had the tiniest hand-quilting I had ever seen, a beautifully subtle palette, crisp points and wonderfully accurate quilting patterns. All made by hand in an era when there was no electricity, no rotary cutters, no cutting mats. Whenever I feel at a bit of a loss and have a quilting query, I find myself thinking about how these pioneer ladies would have tackled the problem, or how the Weardale Quilters would approach it. Carefully thought through, I have invariably come to a satisfactory and satisfying conclusion.

Focusing on friends, not gadgets

I have met up with some local ladies on the island where I now live (Terceira, Azores) and we are going to form our own quilting group. We'll probably be doing traditional block patchwork, either by hand or machine, but we won't have the latest gadgets.

It's expensive getting things to the Azores, partly because of the postal charges and customs duties, but also because the ladies do not have much by way of disposable income. We're not too fazed by that. We've already made Somerset Patchwork fabric boxes and our next joint venture is going to be Japanese Folded Patchwork. It'll be fun.

Note from the editor:

Linda didn't mention it, but she has written and published two books about her travels, so if you'd like to read more you can find her books 'Trip Around the World: A Circumnavigation in Journal Quilts' and "Fair Winds and Safe Passage" on Amazon.

Further reading

Our online book club

By Nina Danielsson

Did you know that we have our own online book club for quilting and sewing related books and that everyone is welcome to join? Just head over to our website, ukqu.co.uk, to see the books we are suggesting every month.

Join us to read and discuss fictional quilting or sewing themed novels by e.g. Tracy Chevalier, Elizabeth Lynn Casey and Liz Trenow, as well as books with more of a political or historical theme, written by e.g. Gayle Lemmon, Whitney Otto and Sara Tuvel Bernstein.

Our first book

Our first book, UK Quilters United by a common thread, was collated and edited by Julie Passey. Unfortunately, the original edition of 100 copies has sold out, but thanks to Julie's generosity we've been able to make two new editions available on Amazon; a Kindle version with text only, and a paperback version which includes full-colour images and the original instructions for The Quilted Kingdom by AbbieAnne Searle. Thanks Julie and Abbie!

Find the book club at ukqu.co.uk/tag/bookclub/
Find Nina at www.instagram.com/bossyoz

Printed in Great Britain
by Amazon